IMAGES
of America

LESBIAN AND GAY
RICHMOND

ILLUSTRATION OF MARY READ (RIGHT) AND ANNE BONNY. Accounts suggest that female pirates Anne Bonny and Mary Read (*c.* 1690–1721) may have entered into a romantic relationship aboard Pirate "Calico Jack" Rackham's ship. These two 18th-century pirates fought and plundered from the Caribbean to New England and so came along the Virginia coast.

IMAGES
of America

LESBIAN AND GAY
RICHMOND

Beth Marschak and Alex Lorch

ARCADIA
PUBLISHING

Published by Arcadia Publishing
Charleston SC, Chicago IL, Portsmouth NH, San Francisco CA

Library of Congress Catalog Card Number: 2007939612

For all general information contact Arcadia Publishing at:
Telephone 843-853-2070
Fax 843-853-0044
E-mail sales@arcadiapublishing.com
For customer service and orders:
Toll-Free 1-888-313-2665

Visit us on the Internet at www.arcadiapublishing.com

To Richmond LGBT families and their friends.

CONTENTS

ACKNOWLEDGMENTS

If not for Virginia Commonwealth University (VCU) Libraries' recent decision to preserve the history and archives of gays, lesbians, bisexuals, transgenders, and other under-documented Virginians, this book may have been printed many years from now. Begun as part of a National Historical Publications and Records Commission grant, the Archives of the New Dominion at VCU Libraries now houses the largest collection of Virginia-related gay and lesbian historical materials in the commonwealth. The LGBT collections at VCU Libraries dispensed invaluable information and numerous photographs for use in this book.

The authors extend their thanks to those in the community who verified facts, retold anecdotes, and contributed dozens of photographs to augment the story of what would have been a less complete history. Notable contributors included Carl Archacki, Betsy Brinson, Mary Dean Carter, Kenneth Decker, the Fan Free Clinic, Walter Foery, Bruce Garnett, C. J. George, Ted Heck, Gene Hulbert, Mary Gay Hutcherson, Suzanne Keller, Stanley Kelsey, Guy Kinman, Lana R. Lawrence, Matt Manion, the Mulberry House family, Ed Peeples, Judd Proctor, Marc Purintun, Stanley Rothenberg, David Stover, Bob Swisher, Tracy Thorne-Begland, Jim Todd and Phoenix Rising bookstore, Anita Smith, Jeff Trollinger, Bobbi Weinstock, and Richmond Lesbian-Feminists. We also wish to thank Charles Saunders and the staff of the *Richmond Times-Dispatch* archives, the University of Richmond Law Library, the Richmond Public Library reference desk, and Valentine Richmond History Center tour guides. The authors also benefited from the immense logistical support of Brooksi Hudson at Arcadia Publishing.

A special thank-you is extended to VCU Libraries' staff and in particular their Special Collections and Archives staff of Gay Acompañado, Ray Bonis, Cindy Jackson, Jodi Koste, and Curtis Lyons. We reserve our deepest gratitude for our family, friends, and colleagues who have been patient and provided good advice during this process. Unless otherwise stated, all photographs are courtesy of Virginia Commonwealth University Library, Special Collections and Archives. Appearance in this book does not imply that any one person is lesbian, gay, transgender, or bisexual.

INTRODUCTION

The selective images and captions in this book unlock the vault containing all of the subjects and stories of Richmond's lesbian, gay, bisexual, and transgender (LGBT) history. One need only read about Richard Cornish in the *Minutes of the Council and General Court of Colonial Virginia* to find evidence that heterosexuals had company during the earliest years of the English in America. But despite the ubiquitous, if often hidden, presence of LGBTs throughout Virginia history, no comprehensive study of these people exists. This book intends to inspire an academic account of the challenges and victories of these unique characters and their enduring legacy on civil rights.

Several Richmonders in this book, including Hunter Stagg (1895–1960), Adele Clark (1882–1983), and Mary Dallas Street (1885–1951), lived during a time of changing societal perceptions of same-sex relationships. In the late 19th century, close friendships, intimate business partnerships, and even companionships between members of the same sex were acceptable. Love and affection between two women or two men did not necessarily imply a sexual relationship but rather a preference to be in the company of the same sex. Particularly in the South, almost all of these relationships existed without an acknowledged sexual component. By the 1920s and 1930s, cultural skeptics began to suspect that these relationships might be sexual. To classify Richmonders utilizing contemporary terms such as "lesbian" and "gay" prior to this period requires evidence that may not be forthcoming. What is more important to recognize is that these intimate same-sex relationships of yesterday bore the foundation for the lesbian and gay relationships and families of today.

Some of Richmond's most laurelled figures and places make an appearance in "Hiding Out," an era spanning from the Colonial period to Richmond's initial period of LGBT activism. In this first chapter are Lewis Ginter (1824–1897), Broad Street Station, and the Loew's Theatre. Their stories and several others offer a first glimpse of a culture and a set of laws that deprived sexual minorities of honest personal expression and the open use of private and public space. Imbedded in this chapter also are the first signs of the "A List" and "B List." While some wealthy Richmonders like Ellen Glasgow could host high-end women's parties in their large homes, many women and men who wanted the company of the same sex were relegated to seedy backroom bars and dark basement hotel bathrooms. Over three decades after Richmond's first gay and lesbian organizations formed, the phenomenon of being "closeted" or on the "down low" continues to claim the psyches of Richmond LGBTs.

Chapter two—"Speaking Out"—begins with the arrival of Gonzalo "Tony" Segura (1919–1991) to Richmond from New York City in 1959. Segura was Richmond's first gay activist. As an openly gay man, he attempted to found a Richmond chapter of the Mattachine Society in the early 1960s. But gay activism in 1960s Richmond mostly entailed challenging the anti-gay Alcohol and Beverage Control code that prohibited the sale of spirits to homosexuals. The actions of gay men following the forced closure of Renee's and Rathskeller's in March 1969 foreshadowed the significant events at the Stonewall Inn in New York City in June of that year.

The Stonewall Inn riots between LGBTs and police lit the powder-keg fuse for LGBT activism in cities across the world, and Richmond was no exception. By 1971, Richmond organizations were active and a few gays and lesbians were outing themselves. The stiff link between the feminist movement of the 1960s and the formation of Richmond's LGBT organizations differentiates Richmond from other cities' activist development. A speech in Richmond by feminist author Rita Mae Brown inspired the city's first formal gay organization, Gay Awareness in Perspective. Members of the Virginia Women's Political Caucus, the Richmond Women's Center, and Richmond Lesbian-Feminists were integral to the organizing of the first gay rights protest at Monroe Park in 1977.

Chapter three—"Living Out"—provides a snapshot view into the recent era of heightened visibility for Richmond lesbian, gays, transgenders, and bisexuals. This last chapter begins with one man's defiance of the military's "Don't Ask, Don't Tell" policy in 1992 and ends with a group of hundreds of "Vote No" proponents on the steps of the Virginia State Capitol. Since 1992, Richmond LGBTs have come out in increasing numbers. Many of them also have begun to advocate for changes in a culture and a system of laws that places restrictions on their life and freedom.

The photographs and captions in Images of America: *Lesbian and Gay Richmond* present the first show-and-tell of the history of Richmond LGBTs. There is pride in this history. One will not be able to watch Robin Williams portray Patch Adams without thinking, "That doctor was the first person to publicly protest an anti-gay action in Richmond." By knowing and investigating the facts in *Lesbian and Gay Richmond*, all Richmond LGBTs move one step closer to living out of the closet.

One

HIDING OUT

TESTIMONY IN THE SODOMY CASE OF RICHARD CORNISH, 1624. In 1624, Virginia executed Richard William Cornish, the first person recorded to have been executed for sodomy in what would become the United States. Cornish was a James River ship captain and stood accused of attempted sodomy with William Couse, a 29-year-old indentured servant on the ship *Ambrose*. At trial, Couse testified that Cornish had tried to sodomize him while the ship was anchored in the James River. On that evidence and little else, the court sentenced Cornish to die. Several months after Cornish's execution, his brother Jeffrey and several close comrades of the sea captain vehemently protested the court's ruling. In December 1625, they brought forth two witnesses—Edward Nevell and Thomas Hatch—who contradicted Couse's testimony. The court concluded that Nevell and Hatch were lying and sentenced them harshly. Both were pilloried. Nevell lost both his ears; Hatch lost one. Hatch also was whipped. (Courtesy Library of Congress, Thomas Jefferson Papers.)

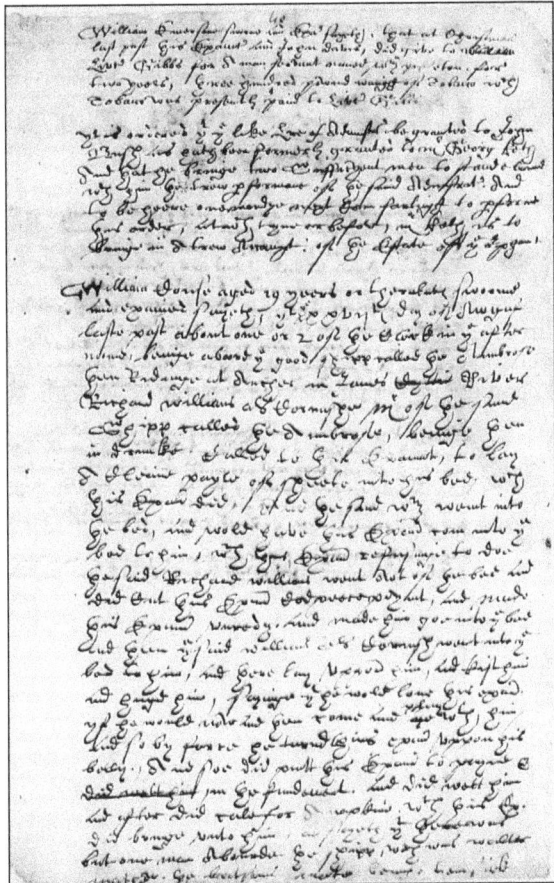

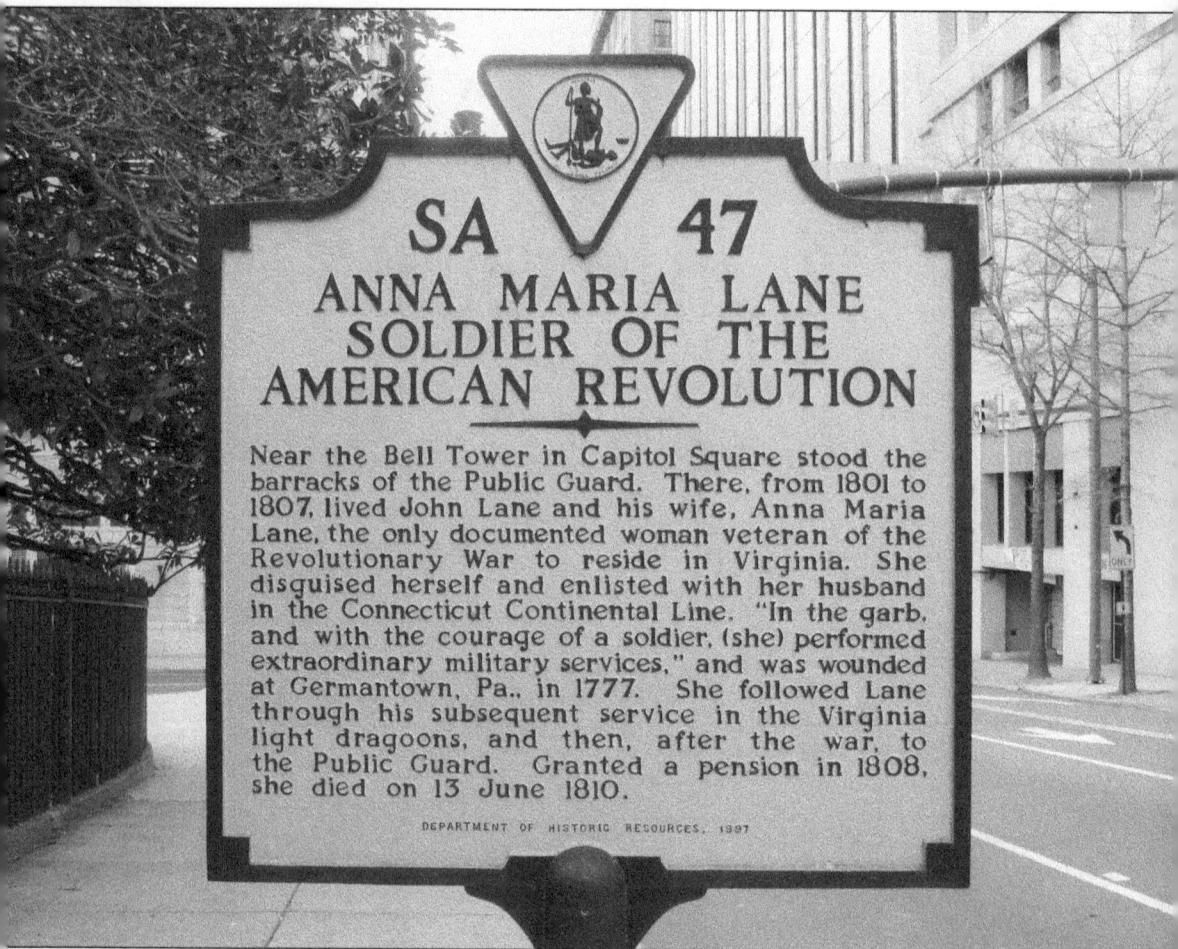

ANNA MARIA LANE HISTORICAL MARKER. Anna Maria Lane was not the only woman disguised "in the garb" to serve in the military. Other examples include Mary and Mollie Bell and Loretta Velasquez, who were arrested and sent to Castle Thunder prison in Richmond. In her memoirs, Velasquez noted that she courted women while dressed in men's clothes.

DR. MARY EDWARDS WALKER, C. 1911. Dr. Mary Edwards Walker (1832–1919) was a U.S. Army surgeon who was captured and imprisoned in Richmond during the Civil War and later released in a prisoner exchange. She wore men's clothing but doctored as a woman under her own name. As a feminist and abolitionist, Dr. Walker was arrested several times for impersonating a man. She was the first female army surgeon and received the Medal of Honor. The Whitman-Walker Clinic in Washington, D.C., which specializes in lesbian and gay men's health, was named for Walt Whitman and Dr. Walker. (Courtesy Library of Congress, Prints and Photographs Division.)

LEWIS GINTER, C. 1889. Lewis Ginter (1824–1897) was Richmond's premier tobacco magnate, neighborhood developer, and philanthropist. For a time following the Civil War, Ginter relocated to New York City, where he recouped his wartime financial losses in the banking industry. Ginter's relationship with John Pope (1856–1896) began when Pope delivered packages to Ginter's New York City business in the early 1870s. In 1872, Ginter returned to Richmond and, having gained the consent of Pope's parents, brought the 16-year-old with him. He later formally adopted Pope as his son. Both Ginter and Pope amassed great wealth over the next 20 years. The two men also would live together until Pope's death. Pope died in April 1896 at Ginter's 901 West Franklin Street residence. According to the *Richmond Times-Dispatch* obituary, "Mr. Pope never married but lived quietly with Major Ginter, for whom he possessed the most ardent affection. The two were like father and son and were almost always together." Ginter also never married, and according to his *New York Times* obituary, he "never pointedly sought" the company of women.

GINTER HOUSE, C. 1920S. When Lewis Ginter died in October 1897, he left a large fortune and his 901 West Franklin Street home to his niece Grace Arents (1848–1926). Arents used the wealth to benefit the poor and work for social justice in Richmond. She gave generous donations to a number of Oregon Hill beneficiaries, including the Grace Arents' Free Public Library, the Arents' Public School (now St Andrew's School), and St Andrew's Episcopal Church. Arents sold the house on Franklin Street in 1920 and moved north of Richmond to Bloemendaal House. There she lived with her close companion Mary Garland Smith (1868–1968), who was a teacher at St. Andrew's School. In Arents's will, she bequeathed one-third of her fortune to Smith and allowed Smith to live out her years at Bloemendaal. Arents's will also provided that after Smith's death, the property would transfer to the City of Richmond to be used as a formal, public garden named after Lewis Ginter.

RICHMOND SUFFRAGETTES, 1916. Nora Houston (1883–1942, left) and Adele Clark (1882–1983, bottom center) pose in the above photograph along with Mae Schaill (right) and Mrs. Frank Jobson (top center). All four women were members of the Equal Suffrage League of Virginia. Adele Clark studied and shared a love of art and writing with both Nora Houston (in the photograph on the left) and Willoughby Ions (1881–1977). Houston, Ions, and Clark also worked to improve women's rights, child labor legislation, and the formal arts in Richmond. For years following Ions's return from New York City, she and Clark lived as companions at 3614 Chamberlayne Avenue. (Courtesy *Richmond Times-Dispatch*.)

ADELE CLARK SKETCHES, C. 1920S.
Late in life, both Willoughby Ions and
Adele Clark were best known as artists
and arts enthusiasts. Of the two artists,
Ions was the more respected by the
contemporary critics and even sketched
a batik illustration for James Branch
Cabell's *Jurgen* called "The Garden
between Dawn and Sunrise." Ions also
has work in the National Gallery of
Art. The subject of these paintings
by Adele Clark is unknown, but both
Ions and Clark often expressed their
suffragette activism through their art.

WILLOUGHBY IONS (ABOVE RIGHT) WITH A YWCA ART STUDENT, 1954. Estelle de Willoughby "Willoughby" Ions (1881–1977) and her cousin Adele Clark (1882–1983) were close even before Ions moved to New York City to pursue a fashion career. While there, Ions achieved some fame as the designer of the "hostess gown." During Ions's time in New York, she and Clark became involved in the national women's movement as evidenced in their frequent exchange of letters. Their frequent correspondence from 1905 to 1958 (see letter on left) shows both women had formed a close bond more akin to Eros or homoaffection than to ordinary friendship. Upon her return to Virginia, Ions did not occupy her family's Innisfail Farm in Northern Virginia but lived instead with Clark at her modest residence on Chamberlayne Avenue. Neither Clark nor Ions married. (Courtesy *Richmond Times-Dispatch*.)

Grand Opening

Monday, April 9th
10:30 a. m.

. . . . presenting for the first time in Richmond, the photoplay spectacle, WILLIAM HAINES in "WEST POINT." It comes to you direct from the world-famous CAPITOL THEATRE, New York City. JOAN CRAWFORD is the heroine.

❧

THERE will also be a program of LOEW'S SHORT SUBJECTS headed by M-G-M News, a pictorial presentation of current events from the four corners of the earth, and other oddities.

❧

THE utmost in music will be instilled into each presentation by SID BART and LOEW'S CONCERT ORCHESTRA—and "WILD OSCAR" at the console of the mighty WURLITZER ORGAN.

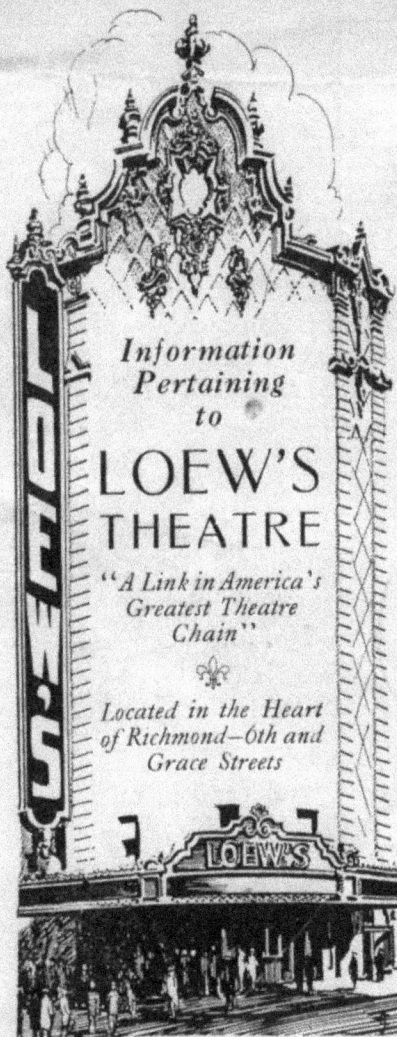

Information Pertaining to

LOEW'S THEATRE

"A Link in America's Greatest Theatre Chain"

⚜

Located in the Heart of Richmond—6th and Grace Streets

LOEW'S THEATER PLAYBILL, APRIL 9, 1928. William "Billy" Haines (1900–1973) starred with Joan Crawford in *West Point*, the inaugural film at Loew's Theater on Grace Street. Born in Staunton, Virginia, Haines ran away from home at the age of 14, his boyfriend in tow. The couple went first to Hopewell and worked for a time in the DuPont factory. They then opened a "dance hall," a successful venture that burned down in December 1915. Following the fire, Haines went alone to New York City. He returned to Richmond in 1917 and worked for a time at Thalhimer's department store. But two years later, Haines again left Virginia for New York. After winning a talent contest, Haines found fame in Hollywood as an actor. He appeared in over 50 silent films in the 1920s and was one of MGM's most popular stars. His stardom came despite being openly gay; he was the first Hollywood actor to come out publicly. Haines also was the first MGM star to speak on film. But ultimately his success did not translate to the "talkies," and he retired from film in 1934. Haines had a second career as a decorator and was well respected in the trade among society's elite. He and his partner, Jimmie Shields (1905–1974), lived together until Haines's death.

LUCY RANDOLPH MASON, C. 1930. Lucy Randolph Mason (1882–1959) grew up in Richmond and learned to use her wealth and heritage to work for social change. Mason worked at the Richmond YWCA, including a period as general secretary (director) from 1923 to 1932. She was also a member of the Equal Suffrage League and president of the League of Women Voters. In the Equal Suffrage League, Mason worked with both white and black women and believed in the power of unions to improve working conditions for women. Mason testified before Congress, and her statements were important in the passage of the Fair Labor Standards Act in 1938. Like many socially progressive women of her time, Mason had her closest friendships with women. Her primary relationship was with Katherine Gerwick (1882–1927) of Ohio. By 1925, Gerwick and Mason had become good friends who spent as much time as possible together. The *Richmond Times-Dispatch* reported that after a conference in September 1925, the two women "spent several weeks camping near Frankfort, Michigan." Sadly the friendship ended with Gerwick's sudden passing in 1927. (Courtesy Library of Congress, Prints and Photographs Division.)

ELLEN GLASGOW, C. 1930. Ellen Glasgow (1873–1945) made her mark on the literary world, earning the Pulitzer Prize in 1942 for *In This Our Life*. She was part of a Richmond literary circle that included James Branch Cabell and Mary Dallas Street. But Glasgow was also well known for her social action. She marched with suffragettes when she visited England and later was a member of the Equal Suffrage League in Virginia. In her writing, Glasgow incorporated strong female characters and a variety of social strata. Ellen Glasgow never married but had many primary, close relationships with women. Anne Virginia Bennett was a devoted companion of Glasgow's for 30 years. Glasgow also kept company with Radclyffe Hall, author of one of the earliest lesbian novels. Glasgow signed her passport photograph (right) and gave it to James Branch Cabell. Glasgow's family bought the gray, stuccoed home (below) in 1887, and she lived there until her death in 1945. The home served as a meeting place for the Equal Suffrage League of Virginia.

HUNTER TAYLOR STAGG AND THE
REVIEWER, EARLY 1920S. Hunter
Stagg's livelihood as an avant-garde
writer, his acceptance of gay and lesbian
writers and artists into his home, and his
lifelong status as a bachelor led to rumors
that he was gay, although the historical
evidence for such a claim has not been
established. In 1921, Stagg (1895–1960)
joined with three other Richmonders—
Mary Dallas Street, Emily Clark, and
Margaret Freeman—to establish the
Reviewer, a literary magazine. This
photograph captures how Stagg looked
around the time of the magazine's start.
The four co-owners persuaded writers
like H. L. Mencken, Gertrude Stein, and
Ronald Firbank to submit articles for
publication. The photograph below is the
table of contents from the January 1924
issue of the Reviewer.

THE REVIEWER

JANUARY 1924

VOLUME IV   NUMBER 1

$2.50 a year   65 cents a copy

PUBLISHED IN RICHMOND, VIRGINIA

CARL VAN VECHTEN AND JAMES BRANCH CABELL. Carl Van Vechten (1880–1964) and his second wife, Fania Marinoff (1890–1971), inscribed the photograph on the right to Richmond arts enthusiast Emma Gray Trigg (1890–1976) and her husband, Billie Trigg, on February 27, 1919. Van Vechten was married to Marinoff for over 50 years, but his personal correspondence made public after his death provides evidence that he was gay. Through his friendship with Richmond author James Branch Cabell (1879–1958), Van Vechten met and corresponded with a number of Richmonders over the years, including Hunter Stagg and Ellen Glasgow (1873–1945). A New Yorker privy to the Harlem Renaissance, Van Vechten took a particular interest in Stagg because they shared an interest in the African American arts community. The photograph below is of Cabell around 1901.

CARL VAN VECHTEN AND GERTRUDE STEIN IN RICHMOND, FEBRUARY 1935. Gertrude Stein (1874–1946) visited Richmond with her partner Alice B. Toklas (1877–1967) and close friend Carl Van Vechten in early February 1935. On February 7, she spoke at the University of Richmond and the Richmond Women's Club. The photograph on the left was taken during a small tea that was given for Stein by the Poe Foundation at the Edgar Allan Poe House. (Courtesy *Richmond Times-Dispatch*.)

STAGG RESIDENCE AT 2301 PARK AVENUE, 1988. The success of the *Reviewer* attracted the era's most famous authors to visit with Hunter Stagg (1895–1960) at his residences at 2419 Hanover Avenue (1921–1924) and 2301 Park Avenue (1925) in Richmond. Avant-garde and gay writers caroused and shared ideas with Stagg at these "salons" until he left Richmond in 1938. Gatherings in private homes were typical of the social scene for wealthy gays and lesbians during this period. (Courtesy Bob Swisher Papers.)

LETTER FROM CARL VAN VECHTEN TO HUNTER STAGG, NOVEMBER 23, 1926. Langston Hughes (1902–1967) was an emerging poet of the Harlem Renaissance when he spoke in Richmond at the Virginia Union University chapel on Friday, November 19, 1926. The night before his reading, Hughes attended a small party given in his honor by Hunter Stagg. The interracial party was quite daring for 1920s Richmond. "If Thursday evening in my library can by any stretch of imagination be called a party," Stagg wrote a friend, "it should go down in history as the first purely social affair given by a white for a Negro in the Ancient and Honorable Commonwealth of Virginia." While Van Vechten's papers made public after his death have confirmed that he was gay, Hughes, like Hunter Stagg, did not speak of his romantic friendships. Phrases and themes from Hughes's poetry hint at his homosexuality or at least a preference for the company of men.

CARL VAN VECHTEN
150 WEST FIFTY-FIFTH STREET

Cher Hunter,

I am delighted that everybody was pleased with the party, but I am not surprised. Rather than quote Langston, I am sending you his letter(please return it to me), but I might add that he was here yesterday and gave vent to more enthusiasm. As he is quite accustomed to brilliant parties---in one week-end up here he met and talked with Rebecca West,Maugham,Walpole,and Clarence Darrow---I can only take it for granted that he had an unusually good time and that he likes you enormously. Do you want to give any more parties for further visitors to Richmond? Charles S.Johnson,editor of Opportunity,and his wife are to visit there at Christmas time. They are older,of course, but very intelligent and charming. However,this might involve you in other problems as they are acquainted with the Richmond colored intelligentsia. Be that as it may you will go down into history. Has John Powell heard of it yet?

The hard-boiled virgin reads like an exposé of a soft-boiled nymphomaniac. I was delighted with your review. I saw Ellen last week. She is furious,naturally,with Cabell's blurb.So is Miss Wylie. What did he mean by it? Emily,by the way,is not a bit perturbed. She considers it extremely flattering that Frances took so much trouble to include her. I cannot imagine anyxxx one who did not know Frances reading the book. These atlantans! George Stevens(in the Knopf office),also from Atlanta, says that the test of social position there is not to have been acquainted with Judge Newman and Judge Glenn! There is further Walter White to consider!

The portrait I am sending you is that of the son of a player in an orchestra in a Newark theatre. It sufficiently explains in itself my reason for sending it.

magnolias and gardenias to you!

Tuesday

Carlo

23

MARY DALLAS STREET AT THE DEEP RUN HUNT CLUB'S HORSE SHOW, MAY 23, 1930. While the photograph is admittedly poor, this is the only image of Mary Dallas Street (1885–1951, far right) known to exist. Street was the only one of the four founders of the *Reviewer* to publish a novel. One author writes that she was "an independent and somewhat 'overpowering' person who made little secret of her homosexuality at a time when most women of her station pretended not to know the word." Street inherited a large sum from her family and was able to live independently of men, an image that may have enhanced the perception that she was a lesbian. Described as a large, masculine, red-faced woman, "Mr. Street," as some called her, was often seen driving her pale-blue Packard on the streets of Richmond. The love in her life was purported to be Gertrude Maxton Lewis, a blonde-locked teacher at Miss Jennie's School. But her love interest would have been known only to a small number of people, perhaps those who frequented parties at her 815 Franklin Street home.

BROAD STREET STATION, C. 1975. During World War II, Broad Street Station on West Broad Street and the USO on the northeast corner of Eighth and East Broad Streets were full of servicemen on leave or en route to new military assignments. In these years and the years immediately following the war, the basements and restrooms of several downtown hotels and travel spots became the center for gay cruising. This activity was the foundation for what later became known as the "Block."

MARY WINGFIELD SCOTT, 1944.
Richmond preservationist Mary Wingfield Scott (1895–1983) earned a Ph.D. in architectural history from the University of Chicago before crusading against a city intent on destroying hundreds of old and historic homes. Buildings that she did not save from destruction were often purchased by the activist. The architectural historian even penned two books about her knowledge of Richmond structures, *Old Richmond Neighborhoods* and *Houses of Old Richmond*. Mary Wingfield Scott also owned property outside the city in Wytheville, Virginia, where she purportedly escaped with her companion, Virginia Reese Withers. (Courtesy *Richmond Times-Dispatch*.)

CAPITOL HOTEL, SITE OF MARRONI'S RESTAURANT. Marroni's restaurant opened in 1947 on the ground floor of the by-then-seedy Capitol Hotel at 206 North Eighth Street. Marroni's was dimly lit, typical of gay bars from the era, and also racially segregated like all other Richmond restaurants at this time. Owned by E. Louis Marroni, the eatery closed in 1962. The next year, the site became the home of Renee's restaurant and bar, another gay-friendly establishment. (Courtesy Bob Swisher Papers.)

TANGLEWOOD, 1988. Located west of Richmond in rural Goochland County, Tanglewood was a beer joint and popular hangout for both gay and straight in the years following World War II. The front of the building included a country store with gasoline pumps, while a separate door in the back of Tanglewood offered entry to a dance hall, pool parlor, and bar. A window inside the store allowed locals to view the goings-on in the back room. In the 1950s, Tanglewood was a retreat following summer softball tournaments for local and out-of-town lesbians. For women who could not afford to host high-end parties in their spacious homes, sporting events and restaurants like Tanglewood were the chosen gathering spots. (Photograph by John Richardson, courtesy Bob Swisher Papers.)

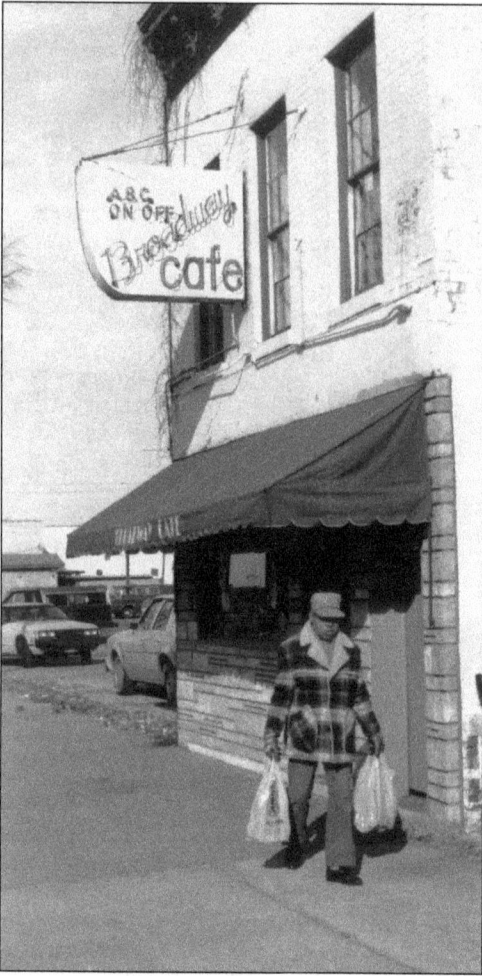

BROADWAY CAFÉ (FORMERLY BENNY SEPUL'S), 1983, AND CARL FREELAND, C. 1997. Opening in 1951, Benny Sepul's was a mom-and-pop café owned by Benny and Maria Sepulveda and originally located at 801 East Grace Street. The establishment consisted of a restaurant (mostly straight) in the front and, entered through a little doorway, a back room with booths and a jukebox reserved for gays. In 1961, the restaurant moved to 1624 West Broad Street, left, where it stayed until going out of business in 1978. Two years later, the Broadway Café opened on the same site. The Broadway Café catered to similar clientele until it closed around 2001. At that time, the building was razed to make way for a home-improvement warehouse parking lot. Below is Broadway Café proprietor Carl Freeland, who co-owned the restaurant with Burt Lowry. (Both courtesy Bob Swisher Papers.)

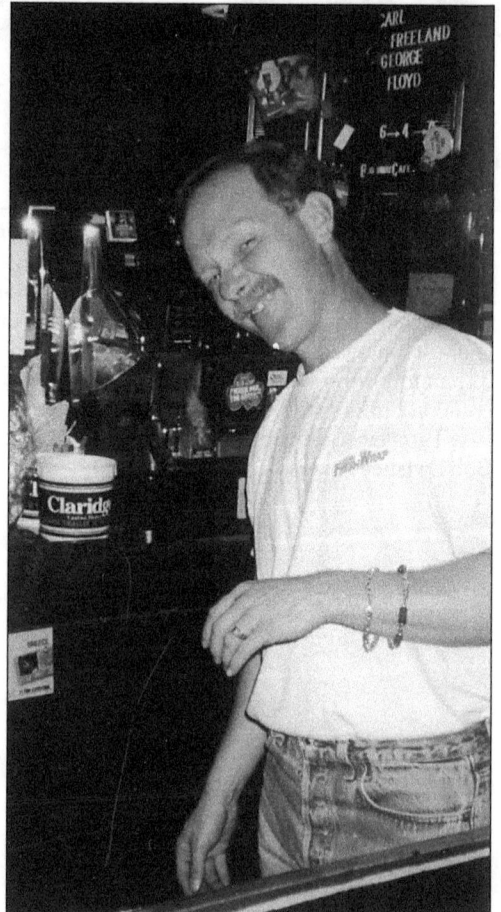

Two

SPEAKING OUT

PORTRAIT OF GONZALO "TONY" SEGURA JR. This photograph of a 1962 oil painting of Tony Segura (1919–1991) by Richmond artist Bill Kendrick is the only known image of the Cuban-born gay activist during his first years in Richmond. A biochemistry graduate of Emory University, Segura worked on the Manhattan Project following graduation before relocating to New York City after World War II. While there in 1955, Segura and three friends cofounded the Mattachine Society, the United States' earliest gay political organization. Segura moved to Richmond in 1959. A year or two later, he attempted to begin a local chapter of the Mattachine Society but found no takers among Richmond's closeted gay community. Segura's activist streak resurfaced in the 1970s when he helped found the Richmond Gay Rights Association. He later wrote for *Richmond Pride*. In the background of this painting is Marsh Haris (1936–1993), Segura's partner of almost 30 years. After Segura and Haris died, the painting was lost. (Courtesy Bob Swisher Papers.)

PORTRAIT OF MARSH HARIS. Born to English parents in Bombay, India, Marsh Haris (1936–1993) blossomed into a prolific author of gay pulp fiction in the mid-1960s and was a pioneer of the happy ending for gay love stories. Prior to the writings of Haris and others like him in the 1960s, publishing "censors" required gay protagonists to "turn straight" or otherwise succumb to tragic fates, such as suicide. Haris's novels *Eternal Summer, Blackpool, Prometheus Possessed*, and *Beloved Electra* were published under the pen name Peter Randolph by Greenleaf Classics and the Guild Press. This photograph of a 1962 oil painting by Bill Kendrick depicts Haris in a Dracula costume with Romania's Bran Castle in the background. Haris and his partner of over 30 years, Tony Segura, met at Eton's in the early 1960s. Like the portrait of his partner, this painting was lost following Haris's death. (Courtesy Bob Swisher Papers.)

Marsh Haris Drawings, 1967. Prolific gay fiction author Marsh Haris also published gay art sketches at a time when the form was rarely printed. In Haris's stories, the protagonist commonly falls in love with a young man with a brawny physique and dark hair, much like in these drawings.

ETON'S, 1966. Located at 938 West Grace Street one block from the center of the Richmond Professional Institute (RPI) campus, Eton's became a popular gathering place for gays in the early 1960s following the closure of Marroni's restaurant. In January 1967, RPI administration officials intent on upgrading to university status as Virginia Commonwealth University banned students from patronizing Eton's. The officials then raised objections to the state Alcohol and Beverage Control (ABC) board about the presence of a bar and gay hangout so close to campus. The ABC board investigated and subsequently brought eight charges against the owner, William A. Rotella. Charges included serving beer to gays and minors and being a meeting place for homosexuals. Following a hearing on March 31, 1967, the ABC board revoked Eton's liquor license. Today the site of Eton's houses the VCU Police Department.

CAPITOL HOTEL, SITE OF RENEE'S, 1986. Renee's restaurant opened on the ground floor of the Capitol Hotel in 1963, one year after Marroni's restaurant closed for business. Owned by Robert Gene Baldwin, Renee's like its predecessor thrived thanks to the patronage of the gay crowd. The hangout enjoyed its best success following the forced closure of Eton's in 1967. Like Eton's, Renee's and other gay establishments suffered from vigorous enforcement of the anti-gay provisions contained in the state Alcohol and Beverage Control code. Section 4-37 of the code allowed for license revocation if the establishment became a meeting place for "narcotics, drunks, homosexuals, prostitutes, pimps, panderers, or other habitual law violators." At a hearing on March 5, 1969, the ABC board heard testimony from ABC agents that they had witnessed "men wearing makeup, embracing and kissing in the café." On March 13, 1969, the board revoked Renee's beer and wine license. The action provoked the first public protests by gays in the history of Richmond. Not until 1993 were the anti-gay provisions removed when the Virginia General Assembly revised the state ABC code. The Capitol Hotel was razed in 1991. The new U.S. Courthouse occupies the site today. (Courtesy Bob Swisher Papers.)

RATHSKELLER'S AND THE DIALTONE, 1978. This restaurant and bar at 3526 West Cary Street was formerly known as Rathskeller's and owned by Robert Gene Baldwin. Gay bars of yesterday were not like gay establishments of today, where people are free to be themselves. Until the 1990s, proprietors of gay-friendly establishments courted trouble from the authorities if they allowed gay spirits to soar too high. In March 1969, the Alcohol and Beverage Control board claimed the restaurant had been serving gays and forced it to close. The act sparked the first open protest against anti-gay action in Richmond. In 1975, the site became the Dialtone, a restaurant catering to gays that was owned, operated, managed, and controlled by Leo Joseph Koury. In 1976, Koury sold the Dialtone to James Locklan Hilliard Jr. Hilliard renamed the restaurant J. Danhill Restaurant in September 1976. (Courtesy Taylor Dabney.)

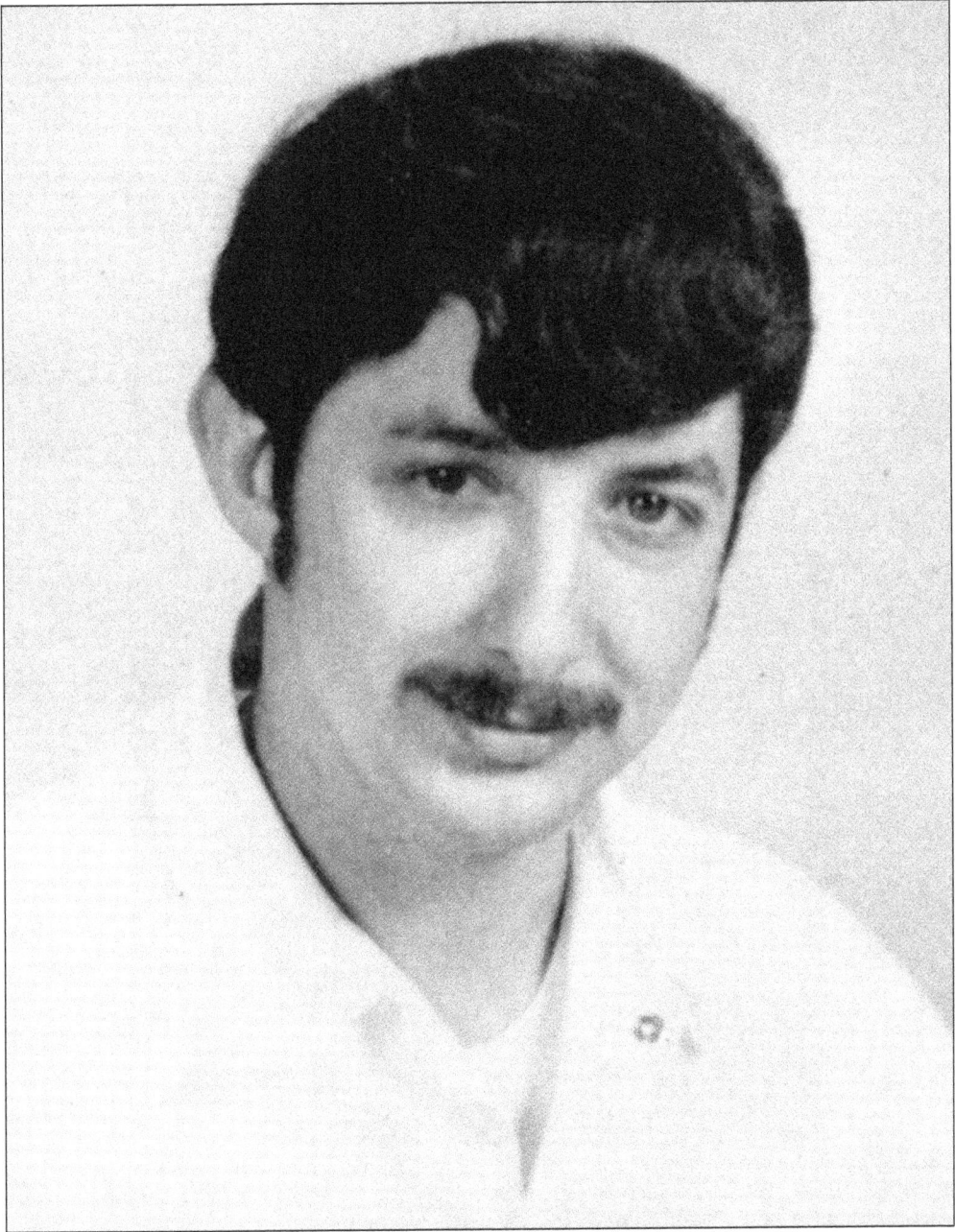

HUNTER "PATCH" ADAMS, 1971. Taken from the *X-Ray*, the yearbook for the Medical College of Virginia, this photograph depicts Hunter "Patch" Adams as a senior. As a 23-year-old sophomore, Adams wrote to the *Richmond Times-Dispatch* editor following the Virginia Alcohol and Beverage Control board's decision to revoke the beer licenses for Renee's and Rathskeller's, two gay bars owned by Robert Gene Baldwin. In his letter, Adams wrote, "I find myself too humble to be presumptuous enough to think I'm more deserving a beer than a homosexual is. I'm afraid that in the atomic powered age, I feel no safer drinking with heterosexuals, especially those harboring paranit (sic) of the homosexual in the next booth." Adams's letter on March 24, 1969, constituted what may have been the first written protest ever concerning anti-gay action in Richmond.

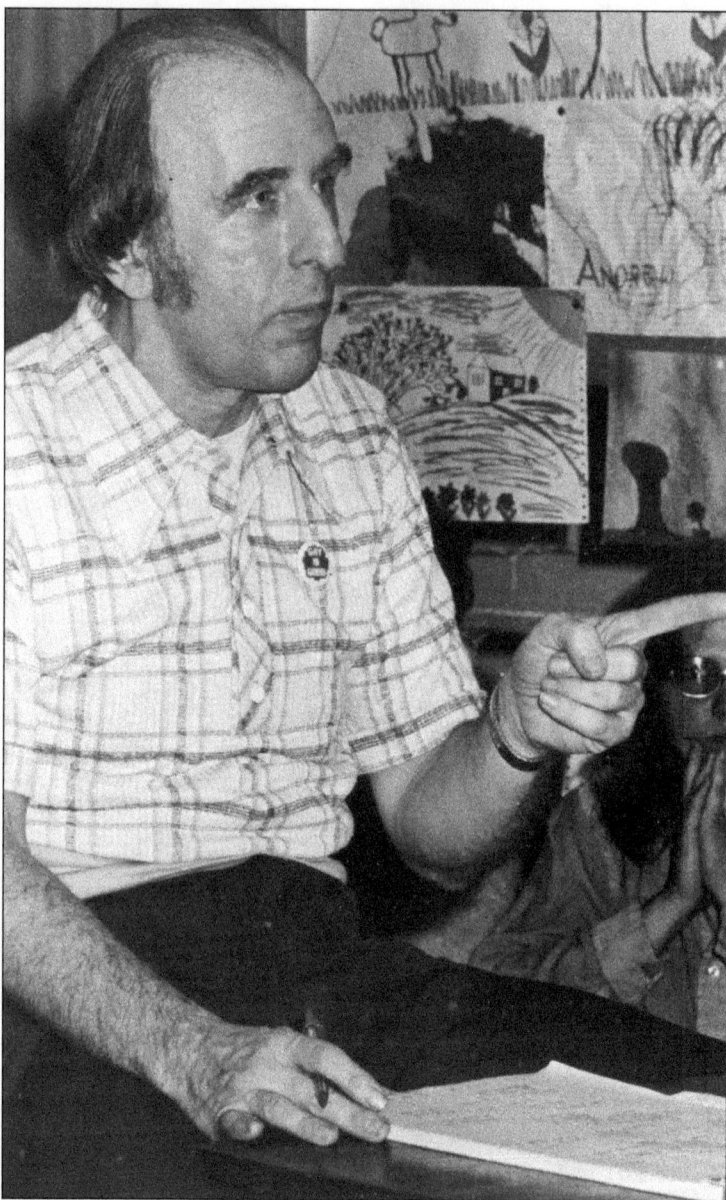

DR. FRANK KAMENY, SEPTEMBER 26, 1974. Dr. Frank Kameny founded the Washington, D.C., chapter of the Mattachine Society in 1961. The next year, he became the first gay man to appear publicly on a national television program without concealing his identity. He also was the first openly gay person to run for political office when he ran for the U.S. Congress in 1971. One of the most high-profile gay activists to emerge during this time, Kameny also spoke out following the ABC board's decision in 1969 to close Renee's and Rathskeller's for serving alcohol to gays. In a letter to the *Richmond Times-Dispatch* on April 26, 1969, Kameny threatened that Richmond gays would protest and conduct group sit-ins at straight bars until ABC regulations changed. The sit-ins never materialized, but Kameny remained outspoken in Richmond. Two years later, he spoke at a Gay Liberation Front event on "Homosexuality: What Every Homosexual Should Know." The talk was held at the Unitarian-Universalist coffee house near VCU. In this photograph, he wore a "Gay is Good" button, a term he coined, as he spoke to Gay Awareness in Perspective in 1974.

'Out of the closets, into the streets . . . the gay revolution is here to stay'

text and layout by
gary thompson
and
mike whitlow

pictorial reproductions by
jim kent

'. . . it's time to be angry'

'When the prison gates
are open, the real
dragon will fly out'

GAY LIBERATION FRONT ARTICLE, MARCH 12, 1971. The Gay Liberation Front (GLF) had no by-laws and did not schedule regular meetings. This informal organization met at the home of unofficial leader and VCU alumnus Kenneth M. Pederson (1948–1991) to discuss gay oppression and plan strategies designed to raise the consciousness of the straight majority. Like gay liberation movements in other cities during this time, the Richmond GLF based much of its rhetoric on San Francisco's "Gay Manifesto." In 1971, the GLF also sponsored at least two dances that were held at the String Factory, a counter-culture hangout on the southeast corner of Laurel and Broad Streets. The above article by Gary Thompson and Mike Whitlow appeared in VCU's *Commonwealth Times* student newspaper and is one of the few remnants of the first gay and lesbian group in Richmond. The group last met in the summer of 1971, when 12 people were in attendance. Even after the last meeting, Pederson continued his activism in the name of the GLF by handing out leaflets on campus, at gay bars, and along the downtown "Block."

MONROE PARK AND VCU AREA, C. 1971. The aerial view shows how VCU's Monroe Park campus looked at the time the Gay Liberation Front began to meet in 1971. Visible are four of the venues prominent in the history of the LGBT community: Pace Methodist Church, the Catholic Cathedral of the Sacred Heart, the original Fan Free Clinic building, and Monroe Park (photograph below).

MULBERRY HOUSE RESIDENTS, 1975. Mulberry House, a Richmond commune founded in September 1972, was a duplex located at 2701 and 2703 Grace Street at the corner of Mulberry Street. The commune included openly gay, lesbian, bisexual, and straight members during a time when most Richmonders were still closeted. Not to be confused with the "free love" communes of the late 1960s on the West Coast, the Mulberry House commune was a family of members who were allowed to be open about themselves to the others with whom they lived. The Mulberry House was one of the best examples during this time of gay and straight socially mingling together in harmony. Family members continued to reside at the house throughout the 1970s and 1980s, eventually selling one property in 1986 and the other in 1987. Among the house's many members were gay rights advocate Stephen Lenton and lesbian activist Gloria Norgang. (Courtesy Karyn Dingledine.)

GAP SHOWS PRIDE IN PARADE

VOL. II — NO. 1   GAY AWARENESS IN PERSPECTIVE   JULY 31, 1975

June 29 was a beautiful clear summer day in New York. Just great for the Gay Pride Parade, which saw Gay Awareness in Perspective representing the state of Virginia for the second consecutive year.

Thanks to the special committee set up to promote and arrange travel plan to the parade, G.A.P.'s representation was larger and more colorful this year. The bus that was chartered for the event was quickly filled and many members took other transportation to meet up with the group in New York. In all there were over 50 G.A.P. members that marched up 6th Avenue under the GAP banner. We were one of the largest groups out of the approximately 100,000 people that participated in the parade.

The committee had sold red lettered G.A.P. T-shirts before the trip north to raise funds for the parade, and they certainly were noticed by the by-standers along the route. G.A.P. members were proud to be in the parade and wearing the T-shirts helped them to reflect that pride.

G.A.P. didn't save all their pride for the parade on Sunday, the whole weekend was a Gay Pride experience. Those members who rode the bus started Friday night with a Gay Pride party at the Doll's house. All present had fun and were glad to get geared up for the big weekend. Arrangements had been made for those at the party to stay overnight and board the bus together early Saturday morning. It was probably this bit of preplanning that assisted with the prompt departure of the bus from the Jefferson Hotel at 8 AM the next morning. Words can't describe adequately the fun, excitment, and brotherhood that enveloped the bus. Several members

did comment that the trip was too short. Somehow the bus made it and after the representatives had checked into the Prince George hotel and had dinner, they were free to do the town. It seemed as if the whole city were Gay that Saturday night, especially in Greenwich Village. Several activities and dances set up by GAA and other groups in New York, in association with the parade, were available in the village, in addition to regular bar activity. There was a lot going on in the big apple that night.

It's a wonder how some of the people managed to march the next day. But they did, for one of the largest parades in the 6 year history of the event. The parade started on Christopher Steet in the Village and ended in Central Park, where there were displays, speakers, and performers. Besides the great feeling of pride that existed that day, one of the greatest feelings that was present was the unbelievable sense of brotherhood that connected every sister and brother in the march.

G.A.P. members marched under a large banner proudly stating our name and Richmond, Va.. Since we seemed to be the official Virginia group, some people from from Roanoke, Norfolk, and other parts of the state joined and marched with our group. Several members of the group were photographed or interviewed by various press agents covering the parade. Besides the banner and T-shirts, the group displayed many, many colored balloons. G.A.P. WAS ONE OF THE MOST POPULAR AND RECOGNIZABLE GROUPS. We returned by bus that same evening tired, but looking forward to next year. Let's plan on three buses then.

GAP RAP, 1974 AND 1975. Gay Awareness in Perspective (GAP) was Richmond's first formal gay organization. Founded in April 1974, Gay Awareness in Perspective met weekly at Pace Memorial United Methodist Church adjacent to Monroe Park. The impetus for the group formed out of a speech in early 1974 by Rita Mae Brown at VCU's Rhoads Hall. Brown had been invited to speak during VCU's Human Sexuality Week by a lesbian counselor who had been contacted by some students interested in building a gay community. The organization's newsletter, *GAP Rap*, was the first news and information medium distributed to Richmond area gays and lesbians. Edited by Butch Chilton, *GAP Rap* published most months until the organization disbanded in April 1978. The inaugural issue is below.

PUBLISHED FOR THE GAY COMMUNITY OF RICHMOND

GAP: GAY AWARENESS IN PERSPECTIVE - Richmond, Virginia

A new organization of concerned individuals who are giving their time and efforts to help raise the level of community understanding of homosexuality. Organized with a purpose and a credo:

> We, as concerned citizens of the greater Richmond community, affirm the right of consenting adults to make their own choice concerning their sexuality. We recognize homosexuality as a valid life style, and we support equality for homosexuality in all areas of living. We encourage the education of the general public and ourselves as to its true aspects. We, as human beings first, dedicate ourselves to service and understanding among our own members as well as the greater Richmond community.

Organized: Reaching all levels of society - A steering committee composed of six members - Three men - Three women - Six committees each with a chairperson - Public Relations - Social - Anti-discrimination - Finance - Organization - Students - Involvement.

The purposes of each committee are to:

PUBLIC RELATIONS - disseminate information among the members and communicate to the Richmond area the activities and goals of GAP.

SOCIAL - create and organize activities outside of our regularly scheduled meetings and committee work.

ANTI-DISCRIMINATION - work with the Richmond community and our own to end discrimination of gays.

FINANCE - collect funds from the general membership and sponsor fund-raising projects.

ORGANIZATION - develop an outline for a workable form of government.

STUDENTS - promote membership and encourage participation from area students.

"WHO" IS GAP?

The results of a questionnaire distributed to 89 members by the Public Relations Committee have now been evaluated. The average age is 24. Sixty-two persons considered themselves gay, thirteen are bisexual, and three were undecided. Of the seventy males and nineteen females who were polled, fourteen had high school diplomas,

forty-eight had college degrees, and nine have technical training or skills. There was a wide diversity of professional occupations as well.

Were you among the 89? If not, come and be counted at our next meeting. GAP is you, and we need your thoughts and ideas.

"Aunt Bee," June 29, 1975, and c. 1980. On June 29, 1975, a group of about 50 GAP members from Richmond attended the Gay Pride Parade and Festival in New York City. While Aunt Bee (right) was dressed in drag, most GAP members wore red lettered GAP T-shirts and carried dozens of colored balloons during their parade up Sixth Avenue. GAP members marched under a large banner stating their name and "Richmond, Va." As the unofficial delegation from Virginia, people from Roanoke, Norfolk, and other areas of the state also marched with GAP. A smaller number of GAP members also attended the previous year's parade in New York City and carried a banner reading "Virginia is for Gay Lovers." Stanley Kelsey served on the board of GAP in the mid-1970s. As Aunt Bee, he won first contest at the Cha-Cha Palace when he sang "Summertime." In the 1980s and 1990s, Kelsey began to perform as Doralee Lewis.

WOMEN'S
FESTIVAL

SAT. JULY 13

MONROE PARK

FLORYNCE KENNEDY
RITA MAE BROWN
MARGARET SLOAN

music by
KAY GARDNER

films crafts
exhibits

EVENING WINE & CHEESE PARTY

SPONSORED BY

RICHMOND WOMEN'S CENTER

RICHMOND WOMEN'S FESTIVAL, JULY 13, 1974. The first Richmond Women's Festival was held in Monroe Park on Saturday afternoon, July 13, 1974. Women's organizations from Richmond and across the state attended the event. Speakers included Margaret Sloan and Florynce Kennedy, founders of the National Black Feminists, and novelist Rita Mae Brown. There were also arts and crafts, music, films, and women's discussion groups. Sloan and Kennedy held a discussion for black women interested in the women's movement. The Richmond Women's Festivals were the first outdoor, public festivals with a sense of lesbian or gay pride in the city.

WALTER FOERY, C. 1974. In 1974, the members of the newly formed Gay Alliance of Students (GAS) requested funds and a meeting space from the Virginia Commonwealth University administration. Their request was denied. In October 1974, Pres. Walter Foery and the other members of GAS filed a lawsuit claiming that the decision of the VCU administration to refuse the group official registration violated their civil rights according to the 1st and 14th Amendments. A lower court ruled in favor of the university. A federal judge largely upheld the lower court ruling. The students, with the financial and legal help of the National Gay and Lesbian Task Force and the American Civil Liberties Union, appealed. In *Gay Alliance of Students v. Matthews, et. al.*, the 4th U.S. Circuit Court of Appeals agreed with the students and ordered that they be given space and rights the same as other university groups. The ruling effectively changed law in 10 Southern states and granted gay and lesbian university students the same rights to assembly as others who might wish to organize.

BRENDA KRIEGEL, 1973. Seen here as a member of the VCU Appropriations Board during her junior year, Brenda Kriegel (bottom left) was a leader in the VCU Gay Alliance of Students. She served on the appropriations board with Dr. Alfred T. Matthews, dean of student life. Matthews was one of the lawsuit defendants in the GAS legal action against the university. Other women—including graduate student Dottie Cirelli, who was also a founding member of the Gay Awareness in Perspective (GAP)—were also integral members of the GAS.

VIRGINIA COMMONWEALTH UNIVERSITY BOARD OF VISITORS, 1976. The Gay Alliance of Students (GAS) filed a lawsuit on October 17, 1974, claiming that the decision of the VCU Board of Visitors to refuse the group official registration violated their 1st and 14th Amendment rights. The defendants in the suit were the 15 members of the board; Dr. Richard Wilson, vice president of student affairs; Dr. Alfred Mathews, dean of student life; and Dr. William Duval, assistant dean of student life. In November 1976, a U.S. Circuit Court of Appeals ruling compelled the university to give the GAS a space to gather and other basic rights.

STEPHEN LENTON, 1975. Stephen Lenton (1941–2001) was a graduate of the University of California at Berkeley and a Peace Corps volunteer in the Philippines prior to moving to Richmond in 1970. Once in Virginia, he began to work at Virginia Commonwealth University. In his position as assistant dean of student affairs, Lenton advised and helped form the Gay Alliance of Students (GAS) in 1974. When the vice president of student affairs and the board of visitors denied the students official registration as a university group, Lenton, at the risk of losing his job, fought along with the students in their lawsuit against the administration. Lenton left the university in June 1980 and went into private practice as a counselor. Prior to his retirement from VCU, Lenton remarked in the student newspaper, "I sit in Shafer Court and know my role at VCU has been that of advocate."

STEPHEN LENTON, 1974. Lenton's advocacy in the gay community extended beyond the VCU campus. He was actively involved with Gay Awareness in Perspective (GAP) and helped set up the organization's first meeting in April 1974. Lenton was also a vocal leader in the Gay Rights Association and a volunteer with Richmond AIDS Ministry (RAM). As a devout Catholic, Lenton served on many parish committees including the diocese's Sexual Minorities Commission.

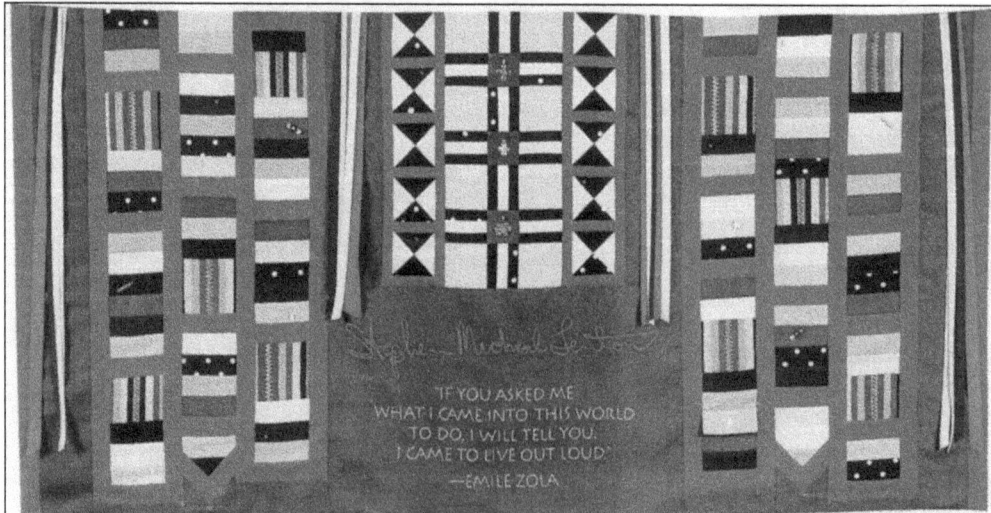

LENTON MEMORIAL QUILT PANEL, 2001. Local Richmond artist and fellow Mulberry House family member Margaret Buchanan designed and constructed the AIDS memorial quilt panel above to honor Lenton's passing in September 2001. (Courtesy Margaret Buchanan.)

JUDGE ROBERT MERHIGE JR., 1978. Seen here with senatorial candidate John Warner and his wife, Elizabeth Taylor, Robert Merhige Jr. (third from left, 1919–2005) was a judge for the U.S. District Court for the Eastern District of Virginia. Named to the bench in 1967 by President Johnson, his rulings in the early 1970s compelled Virginia public schools to desegregate. Merhige also was the dissenting opinion in *Doe v. Commonwealth's Attorney for the City of Richmond*, the 1975 case that upheld Virginia's sodomy law and that was summarily affirmed by the U.S. Supreme Court. Merhige's opinion stated that "private consensual sex acts between adults are matters, absent evidence that they are harmful, in which the state has no legitimate interest." The Virginia law and other sodomy laws like it were declared unconstitutional by the U.S. Supreme Court's ruling in *Lawrence and Gardner v. Texas* in 2003. Even so, Virginia's sodomy law has not been repealed by the General Assembly. (Courtesy the University of Richmond Law Library.)

FREE

For information and help call
423-8291 or 499-3920

Our Own Community Press

Vol. 1, No. 1

August, 1976

Unitarian Universalist Gay Caucus

P.C. Box 6184 Norfolk, VA.

not just another gay group is born...

In this first issue of our newsletter, we want to explain the philosophy of our group. Many gay groups have come and gone in the area without successfully motivating the community to action. Without a solid philosophic groundwork, we also could become sidetracked and divided, defeated from within as well as externally.

We devote ourselves to the improvement of gay life through increased positive visibility. Our minority is unique in that we are not outwardly visible unless we allow ourselves to be. We can be noticed in any number of ways, i.e. stereotypically, detrimentally, or productively. How can Tidewater continue to reject a group providing benefits not only to gays, but straights as well.

The gays who are confused, lackself-confidence, or question their unique life style are gays who must be reached. They must be helped to realize whatever decisions they make for themselves cannot be labeled "good" or "bad" by virtue of a simple sexual preference. Gay is good when we first accept it for ourselves, and better when we educate the public with regard to our pride, productivity and heritage.

SPAGHETTI FOR HELPLINE

In order to raise consciousness and support for the gay community at large, our group sponsored a spaghetti dinner. Approximately 70 men and women attended the buffet at the Unitarian Church, Yarmouth Street on the Hague on Tuesday, Aug. 2.

Discussion took place regarding the feasability of forming a gay help organization. A follow-up was slated for Aug. 10.

At the open-forum organizational meeting on that date, various means of awakening the Tidewater community to the needs of gays were discussed. We hope to petition for federal funds slated for minority groups in the near future. With these funds, the group will activate such programs as a gay helpline, a gay V.D. clinic, and counseling and legal aid for gays. Weekly meetings are open to the entire community and are held each Tuesday at 7:00 pm. We thank the Unitarian Church for the use of its facilities and would like to see all interested people at the meetings.

BRUNCH SUNDAY SEPT 12 2PM

ADMISSION CHARGE: USED, BUT STILL USABLE CLOTHING TO BE GIVEN TO THE SALVATION ARMY (IN THE GROUP NAME) AT: UNITARIAN CHURCH ON THE HAGUE

OUR OWN COMMUNITY PRESS, AUGUST 1976. In the summer of 1976, a handful of gays and lesbians organized a group at the Unitarian-Universalist church in Norfolk, Virginia, called the Unitarian-Universalist Gay Caucus (UUGC). In order to communicate activities amongst the members, the group created a newsletter. The first issue of *Our Own Community Press* was the UUGC's attempt to fill this need. By the end of its second year, the newsletter had grown in circulation and was distributed throughout the state. The newsletter turned newspaper covered not only social gatherings but also current events of relevance to gays and lesbians in Richmond and the rest of Virginia. Over the next two decades, *Our Own Community Press* became known as a premier resource for gay and lesbian news in the commonwealth. In August 1998, the paper declared bankruptcy and folded. At the time it ceased production, *Our Own* was one of the country's oldest existing gay and lesbian newspapers.

MALE BOX (FORMERLY SMITTY'S), 1983. From 1954 until 1959, the building at 310 South Sheppard Street near Byrd Park housed Smitty's, a confectionery and social hangout for women's softball teams. Leo Joseph Koury bought the restaurant in the early 1960s and renamed it Leo's. He continued to welcome the crowd regulars, but by the 1970s, the locale had become more of a gay men's bar and eatery. In September 1976, Koury relinquished operation of the restaurant to a relative, and the name was changed to the Male Box. Two years later, a violent event at the Male Box became a central component in a federal grand jury indictment against Koury on numerous charges, including murder. According to the indictment, on or about January 15, 1977, an unindicted coconspirator of Koury's fired a shotgun into a crowd at the Male Box, killing Albert Thomas and wounding two others. The indictment alleged that the shotgun blast was intended to regain control of the business. The incident led to a period of increased fear among patrons of gay bars as many assumed the culprit to be a violent homophobe. (Courtesy Bob Swisher Papers.)

WANTED BY FBI
LEO JOSEPH KOURY

FBI No. 738 312 B

12 9 U 000 15 Ref: 1

2 tA 01   2

ALIASES: Mike Decker, Leo J. Koury

NCIC: 121013CO15TTAA12CI14

Photograph taken 1977

DESCRIPTION

AGE: 44, born July 14, 1934, Pittsburgh, Pennsylvania
HEIGHT: 5'11"   EYES: brown
WEIGHT: 240 pounds   COMPLEXION: dark
BUILD: heavy   RACE: white
HAIR: black   NATIONALITY: American
OCCUPATIONS: restaurant operator, baseball umpire
REMARKS: reported to be a diabetic requiring insulin shots
SOCIAL SECURITY NUMBER USED: 224-38-4566

CAUTION

KOURY, A KNOWN ORGANIZED CRIME FIGURE WHO OPERATED SEVERAL VIRGINIA RESTAURANTS FREQUENTED BY THE GAY COMMUNITY, IS BEING SOUGHT IN CONNECTION WITH THE SHOOTING MURDERS OF TWO INDIVIDUALS AND ATTEMPTED CONTRACT MURDER OF THREE OTHERS. HE IS ALSO WANTED FOR CONSPIRACY TO KIDNAP AN INDIVIDUAL FOR A SUBSTANTIAL RANSOM PAYMENT. KOURY SHOULD BE CONSIDERED ARMED AND EXTREMELY DANGEROUS.

A Federal warrant was issued on October 30, 1978, at Richmond, Virginia, charging Koury with violation of the Racketeer Influenced and Corrupt Organizations Statute (Title 18, U. S. Code, Section 1961(4), murder, extortion and attempted murder; Section 1951, Hobbs Act - extortion; Section 875(a), extortion - involving interstate communications; Section 1341, mail fraud; Section 894, extortionate credit transactions; and Section 1503, obstruction of justice).

IF YOU HAVE INFORMATION CONCERNING THIS PERSON, PLEASE CONTACT YOUR LOCAL FBI OFFICE. TELEPHONE NUMBERS AND ADDRESSES OF ALL FBI OFFICES LISTED ON BACK.

Director
Federal Bureau of Investigation

Identification Order 4824

Leo Koury Most Wanted Poster, 1979. Richmond native Leo Joseph Koury (1934–1991) operated a restaurant on Lakeside Avenue before purchasing Smitty's in the early 1960s and changing the name to Leo's. It was here that the self-proclaimed "godfather of the gay community" first developed a gay clientele. Years later, Koury bought the Dialtone, a Carytown bar that also attracted the gay crowd. He also owned the gay-friendly 409 Club, a Broad Street establishment near to the rival Cha-Cha Palace. Koury realized that gays and lesbians were willing to pay a premium at places where they could socialize and not feel uncomfortable. But his attempt to monopolize control of the gay bar industry ultimately led to his demise. In October 1978, a grand jury for the U.S. District Court indicted Koury for murder, racketeering, and other serious charges following violent events at several gay bars. Shortly after the indictment, Koury eluded police and left Richmond. On April 20, 1979, his name was added to the FBI's Ten Most Wanted List. *America's Most Wanted* also profiled Koury in 1991. The publicity did not result in an arrest. In June 1991, local police learned that Koury died on the run in California.

ANITA BRYANT AT THE UNIVERSITY OF RICHMOND, OCTOBER 8, 1977. Former 1959 Miss America runner-up Anita Bryant had a successful singing career, perhaps becoming most famous following her television commercials for Florida Orange Juice beginning in 1969. But in 1977, Bryant was thrust into the political spotlight during her successful campaign to repeal the gay rights provision within the anti-discrimination, human rights ordinance in Dade County, Florida. Her campaign called "Save the Children" was based on her beliefs regarding the sinfulness of homosexuality and the perceived threat of homosexual recruitment of children. The campaign struck an exposed national nerve and polarized the subject of homosexuality like nothing else had previously done. Pastor Jerry Falwell (1933–2007), then virtually unknown, traveled to Miami to support Bryant. (Courtesy *Richmond Times-Dispatch*.)

No More O. J. from the Un-Shine State

Miami Victory Campaign-3041 Grand Ave. Miami 33133-Ph. 444-4412

ORANGE JUICE BOYCOTT BUMPER STICKER, 1977. The day after the repeal of the Dade County ordinance, Bryant sang in Norfolk, Virginia, at the Scope Coliseum and was met by gay rights protestors. The protestors included over a dozen from Richmond. Her 1977–1978 singing tour was followed by numerous boycotts and rallies like the one in Norfolk.

51

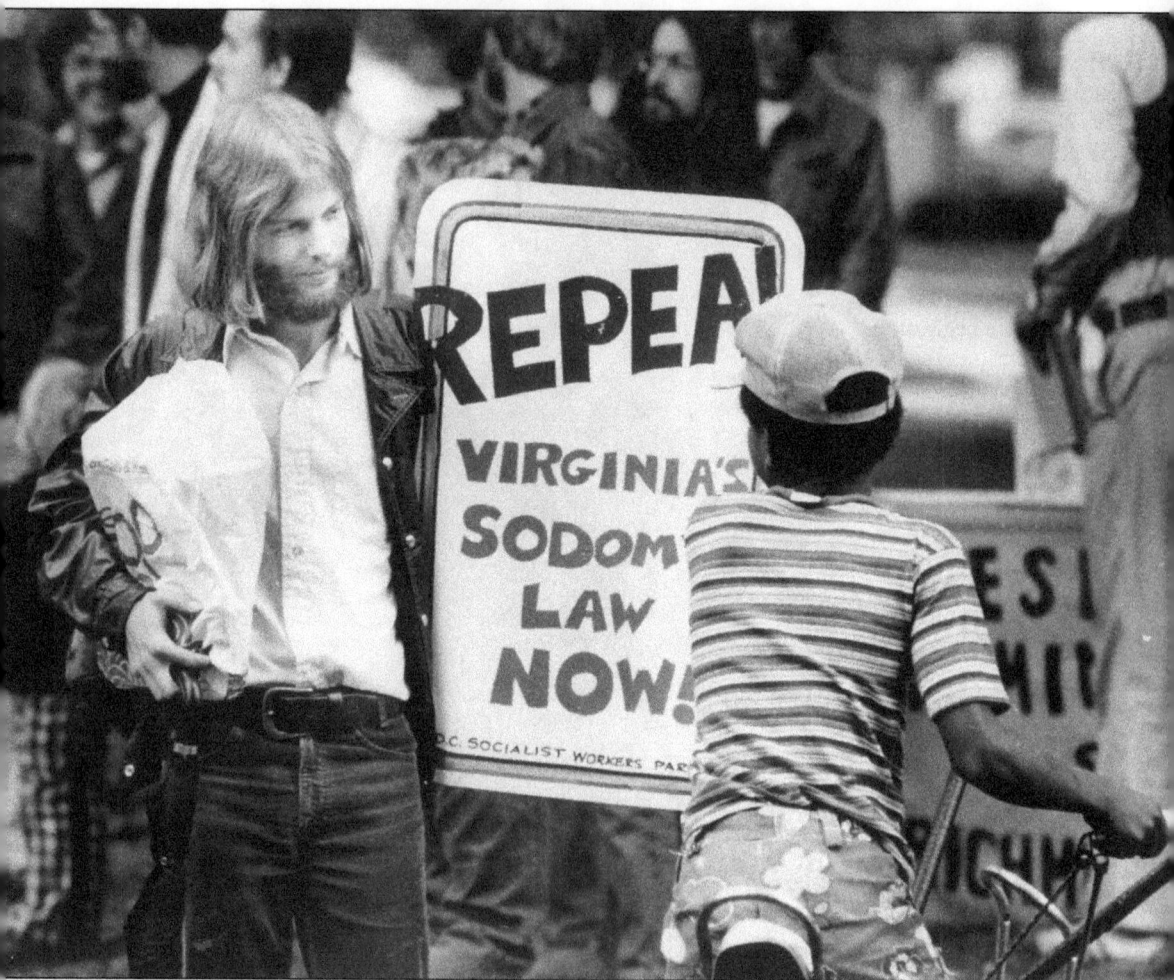

MONROE PARK PROTEST, OCTOBER 8, 1977. Following the June 1977 protest against Anita Bryant in Norfolk, members from several LGBT organizations began to meet under the name Richmond Citizens for Gay and Lesbian Rights for the purpose of organizing a rally when Bryant visited Richmond. On October 8, 1977, Anita Bryant gave a concert at the Robins Center sponsored by the University of Richmond and First Baptist Church. The event served as the occasion for the city's first organized gay rights rally. Prior to the concert, several hundred supporters of gay rights gathered at Monroe Park to protest. The keynote speech was given by author and activist Karla Jay. Rally participants capped off the event with a reception at Pace Methodist Church and a dance at the Sheraton Inn. (Courtesy *Richmond Times-Dispatch*.)

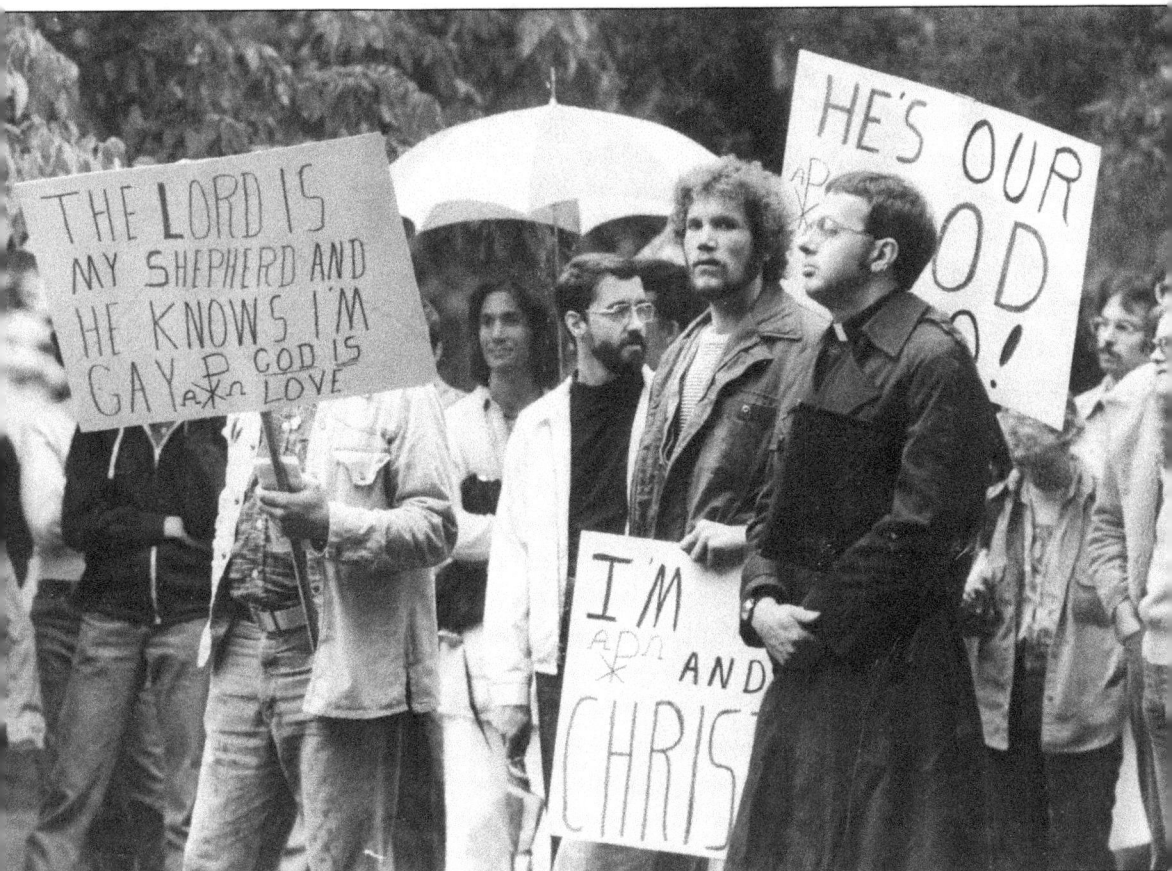

GAY RIGHTS RALLY AT MONROE PARK, OCTOBER 8, 1977. The entire series of events surrounding the Bryant concert and the Monroe Park protest sparked increased interest in organizing for gay rights in Richmond. Two weeks after the contest, the Richmond Gay Rights Association was formed. On February 25, 1978, forty-three people representing fourteen LGBT organizations met and formed the Virginia Coalition for Lesbian and Gay Rights (VCLGR). This was a statewide organization composed of eight men and eight women from lesbian and gay groups across the state. The group principally served as the state's LGBT information and communication network. In 1980, they elected Beth Marschak to speak for their interests as a registered lobbyist at the Virginia General Assembly. She was the first person to lobby the Virginia legislature on behalf of LGBT rights. Bryant's campaign across the country inspired a new wave of gays and lesbians in smaller cities and towns like Richmond to come out of the closet and reenergized the gay rights movement. (Courtesy *Richmond Times-Dispatch*.)

VINYL RECORD OF "HURRICANE ANITA." Lynn Frizzel (died 1987) performed his song "Hurricane Anita" at the rally in Monroe Park on October 8, 1977. Frizzel seized on the opportunity to make a record mocking Anita Bryant and her "Save the Children" campaign during the timely appearance of "Anita," the first named tropical storm of the Atlantic hurricane season. The lyrics of the song poked fun at Bryant's anti-gay remarks. Among her claims were that gays cannot biologically reproduce children; therefore, they must recruit the children of straight people.

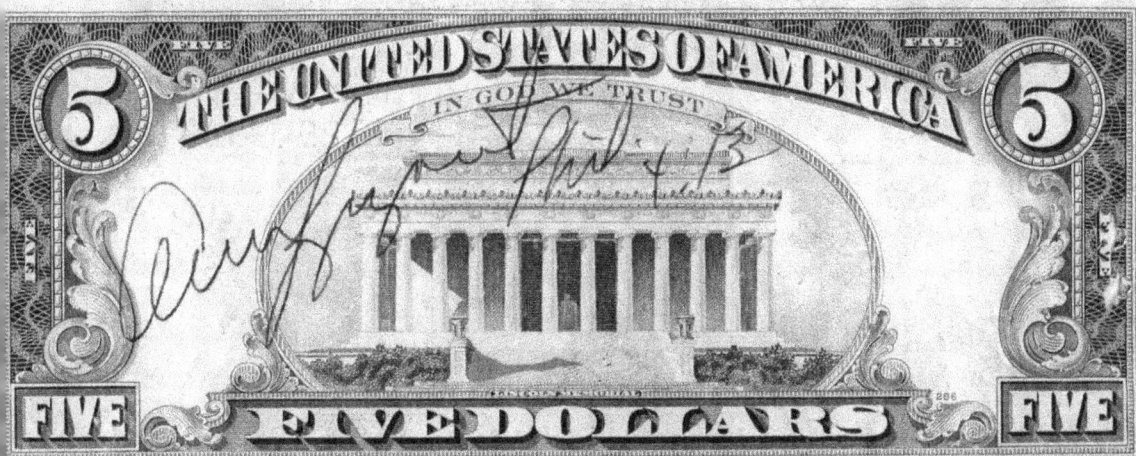

$5 BILL SIGNED BY ANITA BRYANT, 1977. After her performance at the University of Richmond on October 8, 1977, Anita Bryant was confronted while signing autographs by Neal Parsons and Bruce Garnett. Security for the event was tight, but Garnett had managed to smuggle in a "Gay and Proud" T-shirt underneath his suit coat. Garnett took off his coat to display his T-shirt as he and Parsons approached Bryant, who was with her husband, Bob Green. She signed a business card for Garnett and a $5 bill for Parsons. Both items noted the Bible verse Philippians 4:13. Parsons then told Bryant how she was hurting gay people. Garnett argued with her about the Bible. The event inspired Garnett and Parsons to continue their activism. Two weeks later, Garnett and Parsons formed the Richmond Gay Rights Association with Tony Segura. The incident with Garnett and Parsons evidently made an impression on Anita, too. When *Playboy* magazine interviewed her for their May 1978 issue, she mentioned the encounter.

GRA Newsletter

Published by the Gay Rights Association
as a journal of cooperation and liberation

| OCTOBER 1979 | Richmond, Virginia | No. 8 |

GAY RIGHTS ASSOCIATION NEWSLETTERS, FEBRUARY 1978 AND OCTOBER 1979.
The Gay Rights Association was formed by Neal Parsons, Bruce Garnett, and Tony Segura on October 22, 1977. According to the organization's constitution, the group met "to formulate action programs aimed at the repeal, enactment, and modification of laws and ordinances affecting the gay and lesbian community, and to formulate educational and cultural programs to promote the general community welfare." In particular, the group fought against perceived entrapment of gays by the local area police vice squads. They also spoke in support of adding sexual orientation to the Richmond Human Rights Ordinance. Meetings were held at 1406 Floyd Avenue twice each month. The newsletter was produced by organization volunteers. The group sponsored Bruce Garnett, a registered lobbyist, at the 1981 Virginia General Assembly to speak on behalf of gay and lesbian rights. In so doing, Garnett became the first openly gay man to lobby the General Assembly. The Gay Rights Association disbanded later that year.

February 1978   No. 1

N E W S L E T T E R
of the
G A Y   R I G H T S   A S S O C I A T I O N
P.O.Box 13103   Richmond, Virginia, 23225
     Telephones: 320-0683, 355-3666

Editors: Bruce Garnett, Neal Parsons, Tony Segura.

VICE SQUAD ENTRAPMENT ON THE BLOCK

Entrapment, the most unethical, not to say the most revolting of police techniques, is the Vice Squad's choice for its current harassment campaign against Richmond gays. Young and reasonably attractive Vice Squad members, often in blue jeans, circulate or stand in strategic spots along "the Block" waiting for signs of interest from passers-by. It is of course easier if the victim makes the first move, but if necessary the officer will take the lead and try to maneuver the prospective victim into some "word, sign, or gesture" which could conceivably be construed as being "lewd, lascivious, or indecent," as the relevant City Ordinance has it. So eager is the Vice Squad that in at least one instance the victim was an ordinary "straight" citizen who responded to the officer with the popular gesture former Vice-President Rockefeller recently got in every newspaper in the country, and which the officer construed as being "indecent gesture."

As of this writing we do not know how many victims have fallen, but we did obtain figures for two days at the Richmond General District Court: 18 and 7. A Gay Rights Association observer reported that in one instance the cases were "continued" (postponed) due to the absence of the arresting officer, while two individuals who pleaded guilty were fined $100 and given a three-month suspended sentence. We have spoken to two victims who had sought lawyers, but both were advised to plead guilty. We of GRA wonder

56

THE BLOCK, JUNE 1977. A downtown fixture since the early 1940s has been the "Block," a late-night pickup spot for gay men that was "out in the open," as opposed to gay bars and other indoor nightspots. The Block also served the needs of quite a few men, married or otherwise, who wanted nothing to do with the gay community; they only wanted sex. At the time of this photograph, the Block was bounded by First, Franklin, Main, and Foushee Streets in downtown Richmond. Over the years, the Block has migrated at times in part to avoid a steady Richmond police vice squad presence. At one time, the Block ran adjacent to the railing on the Grace Street side of the Capitol Hotel, or "the meat rack," where hustlers and others hung out late at night. As in other cities, the vice squad's mission was to enforce prostitution ordinances, but at times, their efforts focused more intently on gay bars and cruising spots. The Gay Rights Association was formed in part to combat a perceived attempt by Richmond police to entrap gay men on the Block. (Courtesy *Richmond Times-Dispatch*.)

BILL LEIDINGER, 1977. Bill Leidinger served as Richmond's city manager from 1972 until 1978. During his tenure, Leidinger was the target of complaints from gays after a perceived increase in vice squad patrols and arrests in local cruising spots. During that time, the city manager oversaw several city departments, including the bureau of police. According to the Richmond solicitation law passed in 1975, police can arrest anyone for soliciting sex by "word, sign or gesture" or through any "lewd, lascivious, and indecent" act. The law was intended to reign in local massage parlors. But by early 1978, the number of gays arrested on the "Block" had purportedly grown following increased vice squad patrols. In 1978, a proposed city council ordinance (78-176) would have reinstated monies into the police budget for the funding of six additional vice squad detectives. The ordinance, which Leidinger supported, was soundly defeated. Leidinger continued his career in government following his termination by city council in 1978 for an unrelated matter. He was elected to city council in 1980 and served until 1990.

WILLIE DELL, 1995. In 1978, the Richmond Human Relations Commission began forming text for a new human rights ordinance to amend the City Code of 1975. At its June 6 meeting after hearing Barbara Weinstock, Bruce Garnett, and Rev. Edward Meeks "Pope" Gregory present arguments for the inclusion of sexual orientation in its language, the human rights ordinance was endorsed by the commission. The occasion was dramatic as the commission chair James "Duke" Stewart, who had worked hard for the inclusion of sexual minorities in the ordinance, died of a heart attack shortly after the vote. The ordinance was introduced by councilwoman and commission member Willie Dell at the December 1978 council meeting. It specifically read: "the ordinance prohibits discrimination against people on the basis of race, color, sex, religion, ancestry, national origin, marital status, sexual orientation, age, or handicap due to physical, mental or developmental causes." The ordinance also explained that "there are already federal laws which protect people from . . . discrimination in all of these categories except for sexual orientation. Indeed in Virginia homosexual acts are still a felony, punishable with up to five years in jail. The proposed Human Rights ordinance will not change this sad fact."

GAY RIGHTS = HUMAN RIGHTS!!

If you don't give a damn about yours – then don't bother to attend the Richmond Human Rights Ordinance hearing.

If you do care, then come to:

> **CITY HALL**
> **Council Chamber 2nd fl.**
> **6:00 P.M.**
> **MONDAY**
> **February 12,1979**
> **(coat & tie suggested)**

NOT A PROTEST DEMONSTRATION !!!

just attend.

Council's decision is based very heavily on the number of supporters. Come early enough to fill the seats –

before the fundamentalists!

RICHMOND CITY COUNCIL MEETING FLYER, FEBRUARY 12, 1979. The Richmond Human Relations Commission proposed a Human Rights Ordinance as an addition to the Richmond City Code in December 1978. City council held three public hearings about the ordinance, the first on February 12, 1979. At each public hearing, gay rights proponents spoke in favor of "sexual orientation" being added to the ordinance. On May 29, 1979, Richmond City Council adopted the ordinance on a 5-4 vote. The ordinance specifically prohibited discrimination against people on the basis of race, color, sex, religion, national origin, marital status, age, or handicap due to physical, mental, or developmental causes. But prior to passage, the council struck the words "sexual orientation" and "ancestry" from the list of protected classes.

EDWARD MEEKS "POPE" GREGORY, AUGUST 1978. Seen here in front of St. Peter's Episcopal Church, the parish where he served as vicar for several years, Edward Meeks Gregory (1922–1995) was an outspoken activist for civil rights and human relations in Richmond. In the 1960s, "Pope," as he was affectionately called, was one of just a handful of whites who protested racial segregation in Richmond. Gregory's activism spilled over into the arena of gay rights in the 1970s. In 1978, he brazenly held a "celebration of union" for two of his parishioners—Les Mullins and Steve Burns—at St. Peter's. The same year, Gregory also spoke to the Richmond Human Relations Commission, an official city council advisory board, in favor of a proposed human rights ordinance to the city code barring sexual orientation discrimination. City council voted for the ordinance but removed the language about sexual orientation. Sexual orientation is still not included in the city's anti-discrimination policy. (Courtesy Bob Swisher Papers.)

BOOKS & RECORDS BY, FOR, & ABOUT WOMEN

OPENING NIGHT CELEBRATION

April 9 at 8 pm

hours:
tues.~fri.   10 am~1 pm   4 pm~7 pm
saturday   10 am~5 pm

LABRYS BOOKS

8 north allen ave./ richmond, va. 23220/ 355-2001

LABRYS BOOKS FLYER, 1978. There have been several attempts at gay and lesbian themed bookstores in the Richmond area. Labrys Books (see T-shirt worn by Richmond Lesbian-Feminist) was one of those. Located at 8 North Allen Avenue, the store was founded in 1978 by Theresa "Terri" Barry and Joan Mayfield and sold books and music by and for women. The store also served as a meeting space for feminists and lesbians. Seen on the right is the opening night flyer for Labrys Books. The store closed in 1981. Later that year, WomensBooks began selling similar materials in space provided by the YWCA on North Fifth Street.

WOMENSBOOKS, 1981. Women browse through the WomensBooks display (above) at Pocahontas State Park during one of the Richmond Lesbian-Feminists' Women's Festivals. The first Richmond Women's Festival was held in 1974. In the 1980s, the Lesbian-Feminists began sponsoring a weekend event that included music, workshops, contests, and a dance. WomensBooks was a feminist-owned bookstore cooperative that started at the YWCA on North Fifth Street in the winter of 1981, shortly after Labrys Books closed. WomensBooks later moved to the basement of Fare Share Food Co-op at 2132 East Main Street. They specialized in books and music by and about women. Their shelves included many lesbian selections during a time when such books were difficult to find in Virginia. Shortly after Phoenix Rising bookstore opened in 1993, WomensBooks closed.

ERA MARCH, JANUARY 1979. Labrys Books and Richmond Lesbian-Feminists (RLF) banners were carried in this Equal Rights Amendment (ERA) march in Richmond during January 1979. There was considerable debate by the ERA Ratification Council, which organized the march, about whether to allow RLF and other "radical" groups to participate and carry banners. They decided not to limit the marchers. (Courtesy Suzanne Keller.)

JAN HAMPTON (LEFT) AND BARBARA WEINSTOCK (RIGHT) AT GAY PRIDE, JUNE 23, 1979.
Organized by Richmond's gay leadership, Virginia's first Lesbian and Gay Pride Day was held in
Richmond on June 23, 1979. The theme was "death of denial . . . birth of pride" and served as a
statement of pride by local gays and lesbians. The event also commemorated the 10th anniversary
of the Stonewall Inn riots in New York City. A motorcade of 15 decorated cars began the day at
Azalea Mall on Richmond's north side and paraded three miles to Byrd Park. Folk singers, banners,
a picnic lunch, speeches by local activists, and about 60 people awaited the parade participants
at the park. Among the speakers were Barbara Weinstock, Beth Marschak, Bruce Garnett, and
Bob Swisher. A dance sponsored by Richmond Lesbian-Feminists followed the day's festivities.

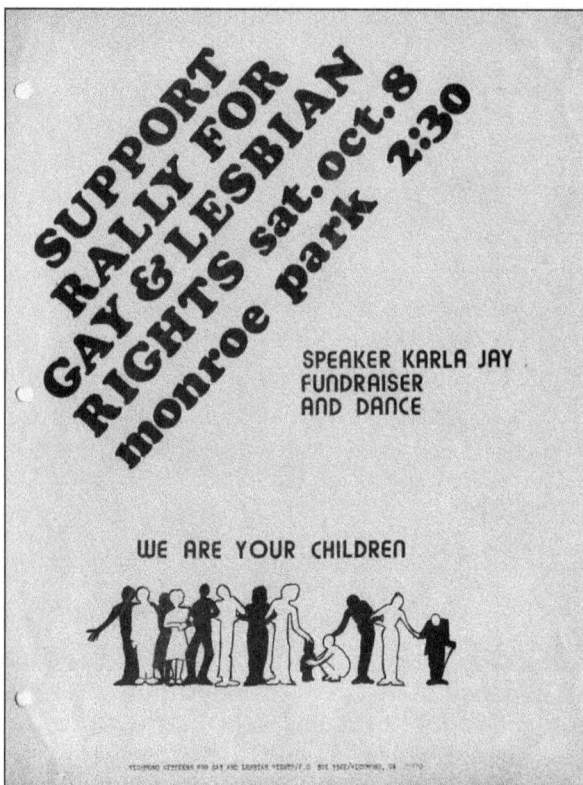

MONROE PARK PROTEST FLYER, 1977. Richmond LGBT festivals have a long heritage reaching back to the 1970s. The Richmond Women's Festivals beginning in 1974 were the first outdoor public festivals in Richmond with an LGBT flavor. The next public gathering of Richmond LGBTs took place on October 8, 1977, when about 250 people came to a protest rally in Monroe Park.

GAY PRIDE FLYER, 1979. Richmond had its first "Pride" event on June 23, 1979, in celebration of the 10th anniversary of the Stonewall Inn uprising in New York City. Several years passed before the next Pride event in 1983, a small gathering around a Byrd Park shelter, including a picnic lunch, local speakers, and music. The next year brought the first formally organized Pride event, laying the foundation for a series of annual festivals.

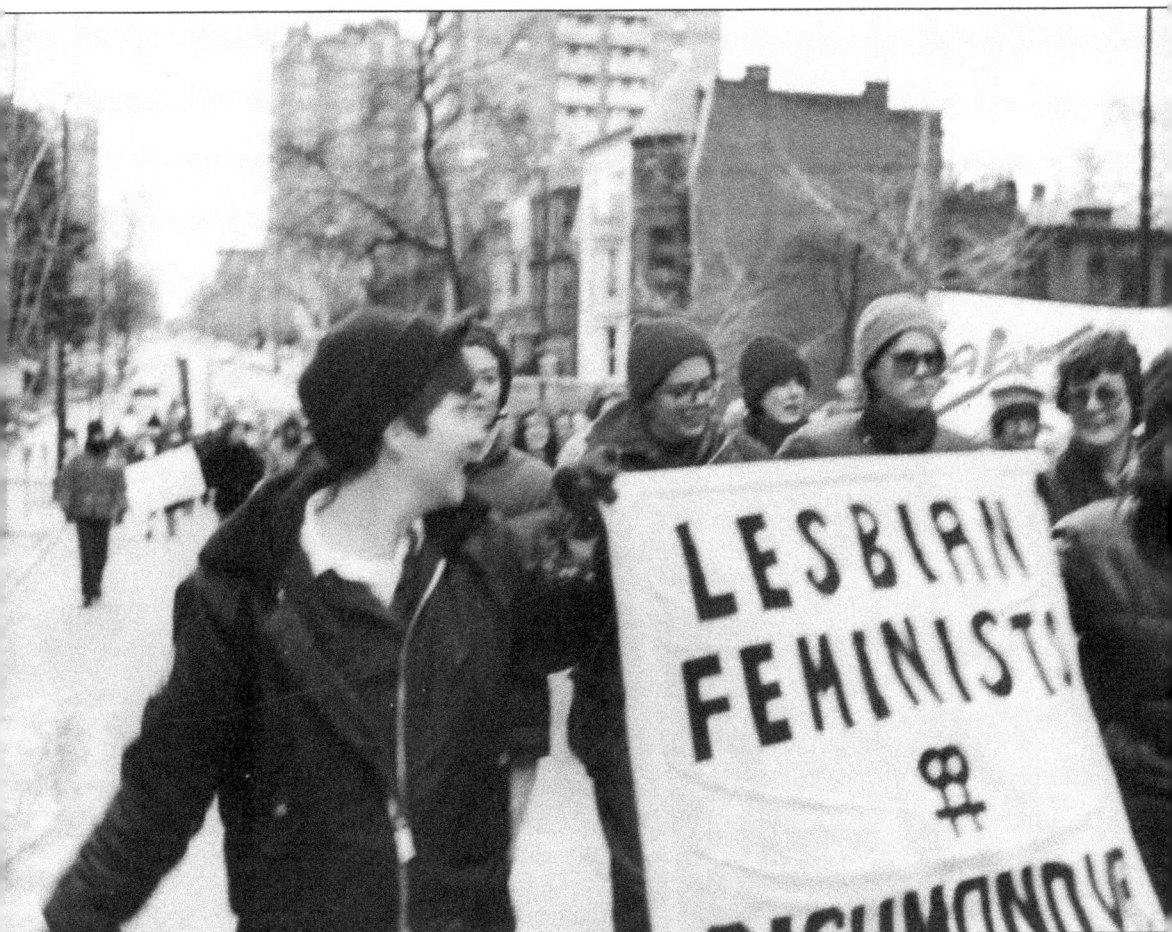

RICHMOND LESBIAN-FEMINISTS AT RICHMOND ERA MARCH, 1979. Richmond Lesbian-Feminists held their first meeting at Pace Memorial United Methodist Church on February 22, 1975. About 35 women from various cities in Virginia attended the meeting. Since their founding in 1975, Richmond Lesbian-Feminists have hosted hundreds of social gatherings, partnered with dozens of LGBT and human rights groups, and provided information about numerous women's and LGBT events. They also marched in the first National March on Washington for Lesbian and Gay Rights in 1979. RLF is the oldest enduring LGBT group in Richmond. The group grew out of the Virginia Women's Political Caucus and the Richmond Women's Center. The Women's Center was a nonprofit, volunteer, feminist organization that provided resources for women's groups. The Women's Political Caucus was a nonpartisan political organization that encouraged women to participate in politics at all government levels. Both groups met at the YWCA building at 6 North Fifth Street. (Courtesy Suzanne Keller.)

GLORIA NORGANG, 1979. Gloria Norgang, a member of Richmond Lesbian-Feminists, paraded during the National March on Washington for Lesbian and Gay Rights in October 1979. Norgang went to the march even though she was on crutches and was one of many who felt that it was important to let their voices be heard. Seen here at a Richmond event, Norgang was also actively involved with the Richmond Women's Center and Richmond WomensBooks. Norgang also lived at Mulberry House, a cooperative housing group that included straight, gay, lesbian, and bisexual people. (Courtesy Suzanne Keller.)

WOMEN MARCH IN RICHMOND, JANUARY 1979. These three women (above) hold a lavender banner with purple letters while parading at the Richmond Equal Rights Amendment march. Many more RLF members attended this march as demonstrated in the photograph below. Richmond Lesbian-Feminists also helped organize the first National March on Washington for Lesbian and Gay Rights in October 1979. In the center of the above photograph is Carol Peterson; Suzanne Keller stands to her left. Peterson later became a minister with Metropolitan Community Church. Keller was active with Richmond WomensBooks. (Both courtesy Suzanne Keller.)

NEAL PARSONS AND BRUCE GARNETT AT GAY PRIDE IN D.C., OCTOBER 14, 1979. The first National March on Washington for Lesbian and Gay Rights drew over 100,000 people to mark the 10th anniversary of the Stonewall Inn riots, to protest Anita Bryant's continued "Save the Children" campaign, and to speak out against Dan White's (1946–1985) lenient seven-year sentence following the murders of Harvey Milk (1930–1978) and George Moscone (1929–1978). Among the crowd were Richmond Gay Rights Association leaders Neal Parsons (center with white ball cap and sunglasses) and Bruce Garnett (front with button and eyeglasses). Four months earlier, they had participated in Virginia's first gay pride parade and festival in Richmond.

Beth Marschak (left) and Barbara Weinstock, early 1990s. Beth Marschak and Barbara "Bobbi" Weinstock served on the Richmond Lesbian and Gay Pride Coalition board of directors for several years in the 1980s and 1990s. Marschak also was a member of the national steering committee of the National Women's Political Caucus from 1975 until 1991. In 1978, she was an openly lesbian delegate for Flora Crater's U.S. Senate campaign. Marschak also was appointed by Pres. Jimmy Carter to the International Women's Year Continuing Committee in 1977. She would later serve as the first "out" Virginia delegate to a national convention of either party (Jesse Jackson, 1988). Weinstock served on the board of directors of the National Gay and Lesbian Task Force from 1976 to 1983. Weinstock and Marschak's national presence in the women's and LGBT movements gave groups quick access to what was happening nationally. In this photograph, the two women are marching in a Pride Parade in the early 1990s.

SITES OF THE FAN FREE CLINIC, 1978 AND 1999. The Fan Free Clinic, Virginia's first free health clinic, was founded at this site in October 1970 by volunteer medical professionals. The clinic was located in the Emerson House of the First Unitarian Church at the corner of Floyd Avenue and Harrison Street in Richmond's Fan neighborhood. At the invitation of Hanover Avenue Christian Church, the clinic moved in July 1971 into the church's Sunday school building at 1721 Hanover Avenue. In its formative years, the Fan Free Clinic primarily focused on women's health and the prevention of transmissible diseases. Since late 1998, the Fan Free Clinic has been located in the Museum District on Thompson Street (below). A First and Merchants Bank later purchased the original site of the Fan Free Clinic (above). Since the early 1980s, the building has functioned as the Virginia Commonwealth University Meeting Center.

FAN FREE CLINIC LEADERS, 1980. Mary Clem, Bonnie Ford, Fred Alpern, and Norma Schanz (shown from left to right) were leaders of the Fan Free Clinic from its formative days in the early 1970s. Here they celebrate at the 10th Anniversary Founder's Dinner at Bogart's restaurant on October 12, 1980. Norma Schanz worked with the Fan Free Clinic from 1970 when she was a volunteer until the late 1980s, when she served as executive director of both the clinic and the RAIN program. The Richmond AIDS Information Network (RAIN) was a program created by the Fan Free Clinic in 1983 to meet the needs of the community caused by the AIDS epidemic. RAIN was primarily staffed by both professional and lay volunteers and provided an AIDS Hotline, support groups for people infected and their loved ones, and legal advice services. The RAIN program began at a time when other health institutions and professionals did not provide adequate services for AIDS patients. By 1987, the clinic had provided medical services to over 100 infected patients in Central Virginia.

SEXUAL MINORITIES COMMISSION, 1996. The Sexual Minorities Commission of the Catholic Diocese of Richmond was an official Catholic outreach support group that ministered to the spiritual and pastoral needs of gay and lesbian Christians and their families. The commission was formed in 1977 and functioned in an advisory role to Bishop Walter Sullivan. Among the commission's many volunteers and leaders were spiritual advisor Br. Cosmas Rubencamp, Stephen Lenton, and Carl Archacki (second row, far right), who served as chair of the commission for six years. When Bishop Sullivan retired in 2004, all diocesan advisory boards and commissions ceased to function until they were reappointed by the new bishop. Newly appointed Bishop Francis DiLorenzo did not reappoint the commission, and the group disbanded in 2004. The group is seen here during their retreat in 1996.

DIGNITY/INTEGRITY OF RICHMOND, 1988 AND 1996. Dignity/Integrity of Richmond was a chapter of Dignity, a Catholic organization concerned about LGBT issues, and Integrity, an Episcopal group with similar purposes. They formed in December 1975, when five people met to discuss creating a multidenominational group of gay and lesbian Christians in Richmond. On January 16, 1976, Dignity-Richmond held its first formal meeting at 16 North Laurel Street. By September 1976, the organization had been renamed Dignity/Integrity Richmond since one-half the membership was Episcopal. Spiritual advisors for the group included Episcopal vicar Edward Meeks "Pope" Gregory (1922–1995) and Catholic brother Cosmas Rubencamp. The Integrity designation of Dignity/Integrity Richmond was decertified by the national organization in late 1996. Shortly thereafter, Dignity-Richmond ceased to meet and disbanded. These photographs show the chapter delegation at D.C. Pride in June 1988 and the chapter's AIDS Memorial Quilt panel displayed on the National Mall in October 1996.

TAXI ZUM KLO, SEPTEMBER 11, 1983. The VCU Alternative Film Committee (AFC) routinely showed foreign classics or art-house-style films in the VCU Life Sciences "theatre," a large circular classroom located on the far left of this photograph. On April 1, 1983, the AFC had scheduled a showing of *Taxi Zum Klo*, a German-language film documenting gay culture in West Berlin during the early 1980s. But the commonwealth's attorney informed the university that the film did not meet community decency standards. His office attempted to prohibit the showing of the film because they believed it to be legally obscene. On September 2, 1983, Richmond circuit court judge Marvin Cole ruled that the movie was not an obscene work. Nearly 800 people viewed the film during three showings on September 11, 1983. The controversy surrounding the film required the AFC to move the showing to the school of business auditorium. The Life Sciences Building was razed in the early 2000s.

THE 1708 GALLERY, 1990. Founded in 1978 by and for artists, the 1708 Gallery unintentionally found itself at the center of a gay arts censorship skirmish in 1990. That year, the gallery sponsored In Memoriam, an exhibit by Carlos Gutierrez-Solana consisting of three male nude paintings. The renowned artist's exhibit aimed at garnering support for AIDS patients and featured information about AIDS as part of the display. Gutierrez-Solana acknowledged that the paintings were a tribute to three friends who died of the disease. Scheduled to be displayed for two months, the exhibit was first unveiled on June 1 in the large street-facing windows of the 1708 East Main Street gallery.

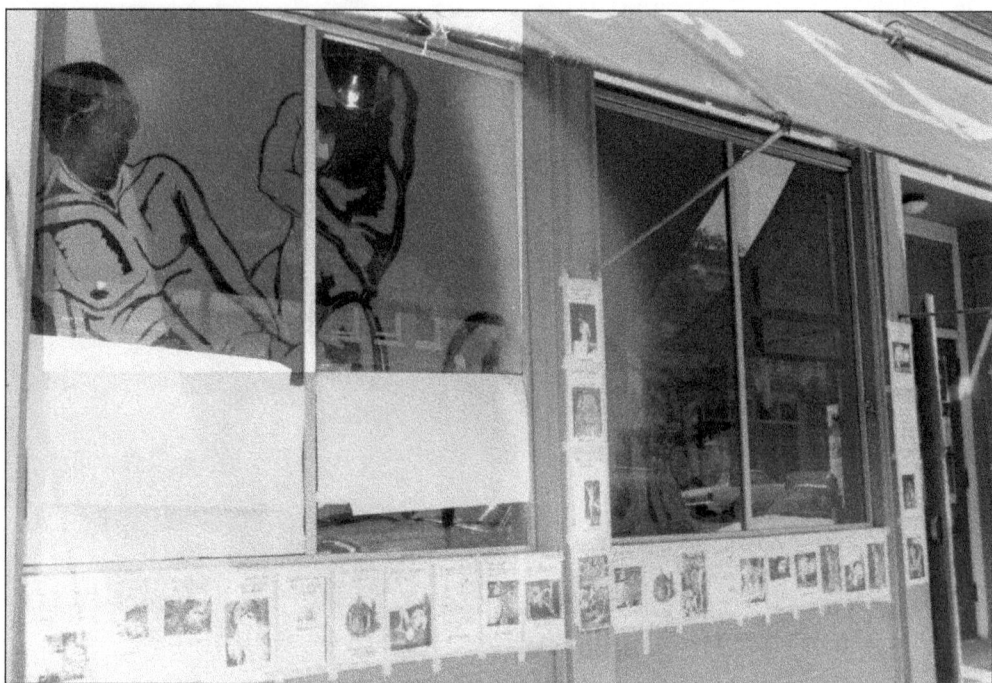

IN MEMORIAM EXHIBIT, 1990. Shortly after In Memoriam opened, police officers observed that one of the subjects of the male art paintings in the window was aroused. The art was soon covered after commonwealth's attorney Joe Morrissey met with gallery owners and expressed concern that the art might be obscene. For a short period, the covered exhibit became a makeshift posting board for grievances from arts proponents and gay rights advocates about what they perceived as censorship. A lawsuit was later filed by the 1708 Gallery and the artist. In May 1992, Morrissey's office and the 1708 Gallery agreed that he would pay $18,000 to settle the lawsuit.

MEN IN BYRD PARK DURING RICHMOND PRIDE, 1984. "Coming out of the closet" was an idea introduced in the 19th century by German gay rights advocate Karl Heinrich Ulrichs (1825–1895) as a means of emancipation. Claiming that invisibility was a major obstacle toward changing public opinion, he urged homosexuals to come out. Other scholars have commented and expanded on Ulrichs's assertion, including Iwan Bloch, Magnus Hirschfeld, and Donald Webster Cory. The coming out process gained a voice in the United States in the 1950s and 1960s following the formation of the Mattachine Society and the Daughters of Bilitis and the arrival of vociferous gay rights advocates like Frank Kameny. In the late 1960s and early 1970s, coming out was gaining momentum in larger cities, but in conservative-minded Richmond, such action was rare. This began to change by the late 1970s and early 1980s following the formation of local gay and lesbian organizations and pride events. By the mid-1980s, affection in public between persons of the same sex was becoming more commonplace. (Both courtesy Bob Swisher Papers.)

TWO WOMEN KISSING, EARLY 1980S. Richmond Lesbian-Feminists (RLF) held a spring prom in the early 1980s in the Richmond Friends Meeting House at 4500 Kensington Avenue. RLF had a number of social events at this location, one of the few places in Richmond where they could rent space using the organization's name. Frequently the room would be decorated with lesbian posters and RLF memorabilia.

BILL BUCHANAN, 1986. This gentleman identified himself in a September 1986 article written by the *Times-Dispatch* about the Gay Pride Festival. By the early 1980s, coming out in the press was becoming a more common way that gays and lesbians were displaying their activism. Recognizing this change, gay and lesbian organizations compiled lists of knowledgeable persons who would be willing to speak to the press when the need arose. Prior to this change, the press had drifted to a select few, often eccentric gays, who may or may not have represented the community well. (Courtesy *Richmond Times-Dispatch*.)

DONNIE CORKER, "DIRT WOMAN," 1990.
Richmond native and common VCU area
denizen Donnie Corker served as the LGBT
voice-on-the-street since the late 1970s. One of
the city's most outspoken and colorful characters,
Corker, also known as Dirt Woman, worked as
a performer, dancer, and prostitute and even
operated a flower stand at the corner of Grace and
Harrison Streets. Corker earned his nickname
in 1976 following an encounter with the police
vice squad. After police threw him in the back
seat of their cruiser, Corker accidentally made
a mess. The cops called him a "dirty woman,"
and the name stuck. At the inauguration of Gov.
Douglas Wilder on January 13, 1990, Corker was
arrested by two Virginia State Capitol policemen
despite having a press pass by a WANT radio
station manager. (Both courtesy David Stover.)

GUY KINMAN, C. 1985. The son of an army colonel, Guy Kinman graduated from Wabash College in Indiana and McCormick Theological Seminary in Chicago. For 16 years, he was a Presbyterian minister, the last six as an Air Force chaplain. In 1985, Kinman, as chair of the Richmond Virginia Gay and Lesbian Alliance, created and helped lead a fund-raising effort for a billboard project. Inspired by a similar project funded in Roanoke by the Roanoke Virginia Gay Alliance, the Richmond billboard campaign raised funds to erect 11 billboard messages in the Richmond area. They were first seen around Christmas of 1985. The billboards (see photograph) intended to educate the public about the presence of gays, lesbians, and other sexual minorities in the community. The signs included a brief message and a phone number to receive more information. (Both courtesy *Richmond Times-Dispatch*.)

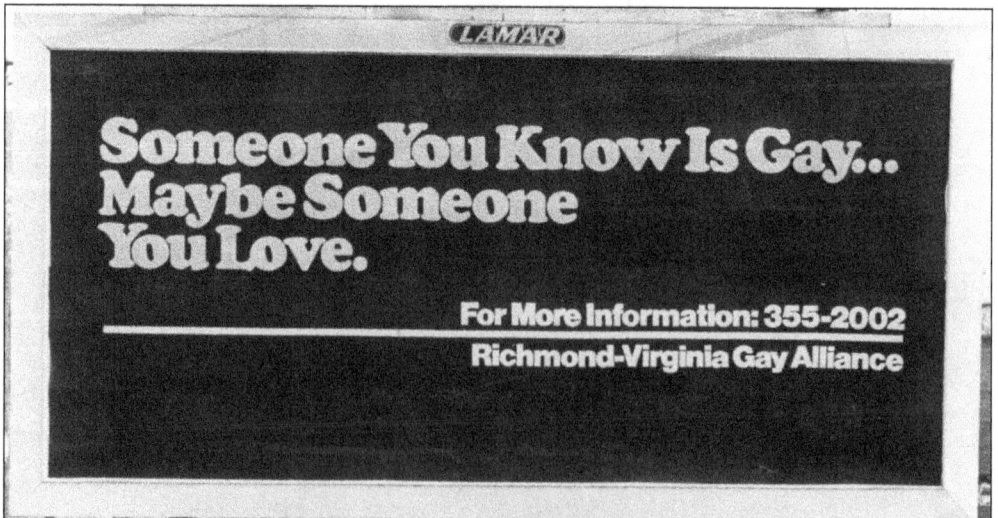

LAMAR

Someone You Know Is Gay...
Maybe Someone
You Love.

For More Information: 355-2002
Richmond-Virginia Gay Alliance

STAN ROTHENBERG, EARLY 1970S. Stan Rothenberg was an openly gay businessman and owner of Scandinavian Interiors rug and furniture store at 3117 West Cary Street in Carytown. His business sponsored an all-gay softball team in the mid-1980s, a respectable feat during a period when coming out was only beginning to gain acceptance in Richmond. Rothenberg was also a member of the Richmond Human Relations Commission from 1979 until 1985. In 1984, toward the end of Rothenberg's tenure on the commission, commission chair Ed Peeples compiled a survey and wrote a report about discrimination against lesbians and gays in Richmond. In his report, 54.9 percent of the gay and lesbian survey respondents admitted to changing their behavior at work in order to avoid negative reactions. Of the survey participants, 84.3 percent felt present laws provided unequal treatment. A third-party company reviewed the survey and verified the report's findings. Yet a majority of commission members chose not to submit it to city council for consideration. Rothenberg's business closed in 1991. He left Richmond in 1997.

The Richmond Pride

VOL. 1, NO. 5   P. O. Box 164 • Capitol Station • Richmond, Va. 23201   DECEMBER, 1986

MARCH ON WASHINGTON 1987

"For Love and For Life, We're Not Going Back"

by Jim Giddings

New York City hosted the First in a series of conferences to be held throughout the Spring of 1987. The purpose of this distinguished body was to formulate and implement all logistics involved with a National March on our nation's Capital.

Only once has there ever been such a historical event so prevalent to gay activism. The conference which hosted over 500 delegates and 150 organizations, constituted the nation's largest gathering of Gay Civil Rights leaders in the '80's. The conference itself was a major historical event. Now the groundwork has been carefully put into place with much work left to be done.

We have our work cut out for us. Now more than ever, every group in Virginia must pull together to help make this march the biggest demonstration for Civil Rights ever. This is our opportunity to stand up and be counted. This march will require input from all groups throughout our Commonwealth.

Among the delegates present were two from Virginia, Elizabeth Marchant and Jim Giddings, representing not only Richmond Virginia Gay/Lesbian Alliance and the "Richmond Pride", but also the State. The delegates had a large responsibility to see that the State came away from this conference in the best possible position.

This was accomplished through long intense hours of discussion and lobbying. As a result of this effort, Virginia has been moved into the Mid-Atlantic Region. This move will enable Virginia to network more closely with the "March On Washington" headquarters which is tentatively scheduled for Washington D.C. Exact location to be announced later.

A march of this magnitude and historical importance can not happen without your help. Therefore, we urge all Gay/Lesbian Virginians to rally and show support for the stand that will be taken against those who wish to deny us our basic civil rights.

More information forthcoming.

ACLU Endorses Gay Marriage, Benefits

The National Board of Directors of the ACLU voted October 19 to adopt a formal policy statement endorsing both gay and lesbian marriage and a range of economic benefits for gay and lesbian life partners.

This statement will be added to longstanding ACLU policy against discrimination based on sexual orientation and against criminal laws prohibiting homosexual conduct.

"This new statement extends the general anti-discrimination principle of existing policy and specifies ACLU support for changing laws of marriage," said Nan D. Hunter, director of the ACLU Lesbian and Gay Rights Project.

"As far as I know, the ACLU is the first mainstream civil rights group to take this stand. I hope others follow suit," she said.

The new policy statement describes both the recognition of gay and lesbian marriage and the recognition of economic benefits for unmarried partners as "imperative for the complete legal equality of lesbians and gay men." The benefits covered by the policy include employee fringe benefits, insurance benefits, income tax benefits, and visitation and next-of-kin rights when a lover is incapacitated.

Hunter pointed out that the ACLU has been litigating benefits cases for a number of years. The ACLU is co-counsel in the Massachusetts foster care case, challenging that state's policy of giving preference to "traditional" married couples. In Minnesota, the ACLU sought to be appointed guardian for Sharon Kowalski, after she was severely injured in an automobile accident and her parents denied visitation rights to her lover.

In addition, the ACLU has filed amicus (friend of the court) briefs in an Arizona case of a bisexual man denied certification as an adoptive parent, in a New York case of a gay life partner seeking a lease to stay in the apartment he shared with his lover, and a California case of a gay man seeking to require the state to provide medical benefit coverage to the domestic partners of state employees.

For further information, contact: Nan D. Hunter, Director, ACLU Lesbian and Gay Rights Project, (212) 944-9800 or Ari Korpivaara, Acting Director, ACLU Public Information and Education, (212) 944-9800.

Best Wishes for a Joyous Holiday Season and a New Year of Happiness, from the Staff of the "Richmond Pride"

RICHMOND PRIDE, DECEMBER 1986. First published in August 1986, the *Richmond Pride* was originally a newsletter publication of the Richmond Virginia Gay Alliance that intended to distribute news and information to Richmond's gay community on a monthly basis. Much like Norfolk's *Our Own Community Press*, the *Richmond Pride* quickly earned a large readership and changed to a newspaper format. The newspaper's first editor was Jim Giddings. Reporters included Carl Archacki, Beverly Rainey, and Tony Segura. Barely visible in this front-page snapshot (left) is one of the only known photographs of Tony Segura during the later years of his life (bottom left). By August 1987, Beverly Rainey had assumed the role of editor. The paper ceased publication in 1990.

BEVERLY RAINEY (LEFT) AND MARY DEAN CARTER, 1988. Beverly "Bev" Rainey was active with the Richmond Lesbian and Gay Alliance and their newspaper the *Richmond Pride*. She worked first as a reporter and then in 1987 became the newspaper's editor. Rainey later became editor of the *Richmond Lesbian-Feminist Flyer*. Her partner during the 1980s was Mary Dean Carter, who also worked on the *Richmond Pride* and the *Richmond Lesbian-Feminist Flyer*.

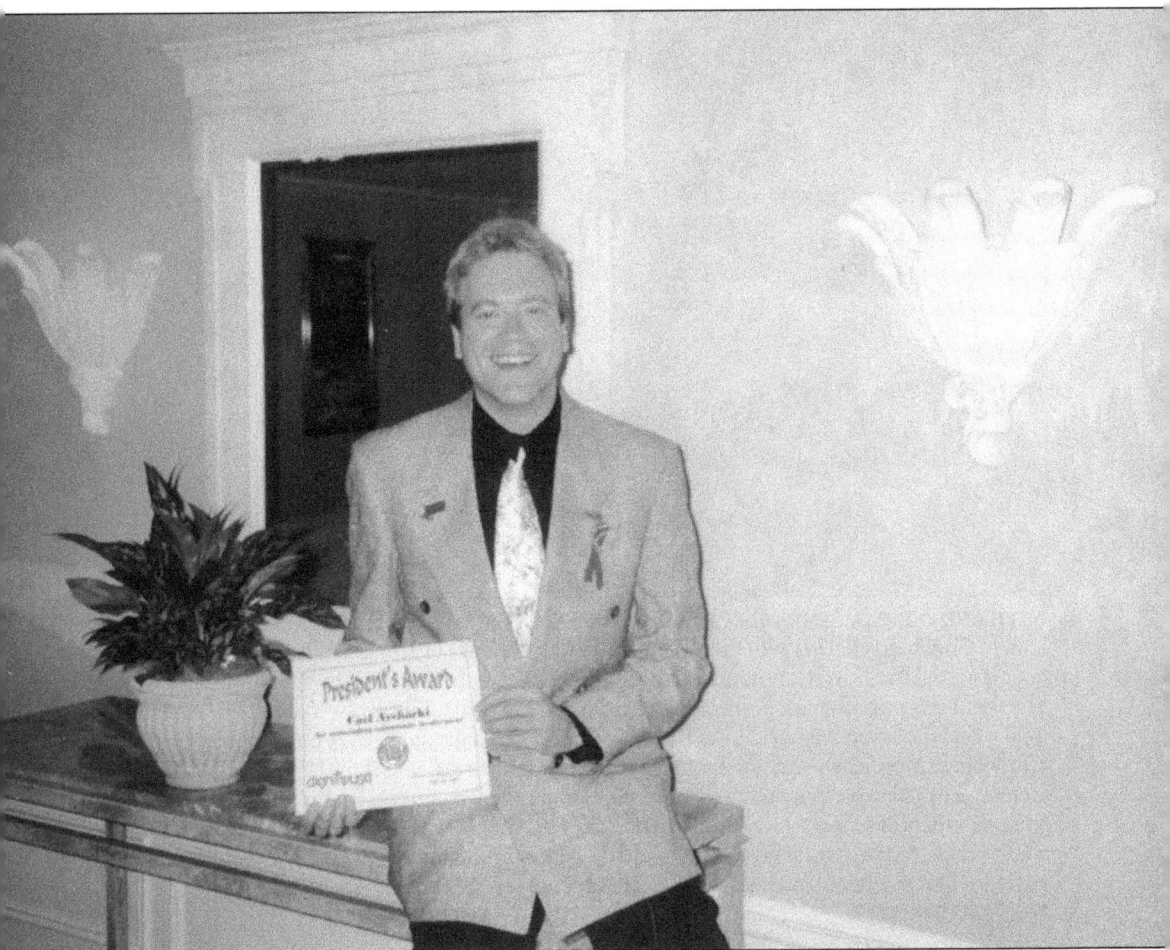

CARL ARCHACKI, C. 1993. In 1986, Carl Archacki moved to Richmond to begin a career in the communications industry. A devout Catholic, Archacki soon became involved in various ministries at the Cathedral of the Sacred Heart. He joined the Dignity-Integrity chapter in the late 1980s and served as its vice president and president. He also worked on the Sexual Minorities Commission of the Catholic Diocese and served as its chair for six years. Archacki helped establish the National Association of Catholic Diocesan Lesbian and Gay Ministries and served on its national board. His activism has included volunteer work for secular groups, too, such as Virginians for Justice and the Richmond Lesbian and Gay Pride Coalition.

SHEP AND NORMA JANET (LEFT) AT A WOMEN'S FESTIVAL IN ROANOKE, EARLY 1980S. L. A. "Shep" Shepherd (1917–1996) and Norma Janet Hofheimer (1905–2001) were an enduring lesbian couple living "out" in Richmond during a time when such long-standing relationships were rare. Shepherd was a pharmacist and graduated from the Medical College of Virginia (MCV). Hofheimer held a high position with the U.S. Post Office and was a graduate of Westhampton College. The two women were early members of the Women's Political Caucus and the Richmond Women's Center. They also participated in Richmond Lesbian-Feminists and Richmond WomensBooks and were members of Congregation Beth Ahabah. The couple was known for their strong opinions as well as their active involvement. Shepherd died in February 1996. Hofheimer spent her remaining years in Texas, where she died in 2001. (Both courtesy Suzanne Keller.)

RICHMOND AIDS MINISTRY STAFF AND VOLUNTEERS, C. 1992 AND 2001. Richmond AIDS Ministry (RAM) was a nonprofit, interfaith, volunteer-based organization responding to the needs of Richmonders with HIV and AIDS. Founded in the mid-1980s, the organization coordinated two guesthouses, a legal clinic, an emergency fund, and pastoral care during a time when these needs were in high demand by patients and families. Seen here is the staff (top) of RAM, including John Baumann, executive director. Baumann served as RAM's director until the group dissolved in the mid-1990s. At that time, many of the organization's programs were absorbed by the Fan Free Clinic. On the bottom are former RAM staff and volunteers Betsy Brinson (in front) with, from left to right, Kathleen Kinney, John Elliott, Stephen Lenton, and Ronnie Moseberth in April 2001.

DR. LISA KAPLOWITZ. When Dr. Lisa Kaplowitz moved to Richmond in the early 1980s, AIDS patients were only beginning to appear in hospitals and doctor's offices. (In July 1983, at least six cases of AIDS had been reported in Richmond.) Trained in the treatment of infectious diseases, Kaplowitz found herself on the front lines of an epidemic few physicians knew how to treat. She established the AIDS Program at the Medical College of Virginia in 1986 to address the lack of medical information and care for patients in Virginia. At the time, only volunteer organizations like RAIN were dealing with HIV and AIDS. In 1989, she was a gubernatorial appointee to the AIDS Legislative Subcommittee of the General Assembly, a body that developed all AIDS-related legislation over the next decade. Kaplowitz also has published widely on HIV and AIDS.

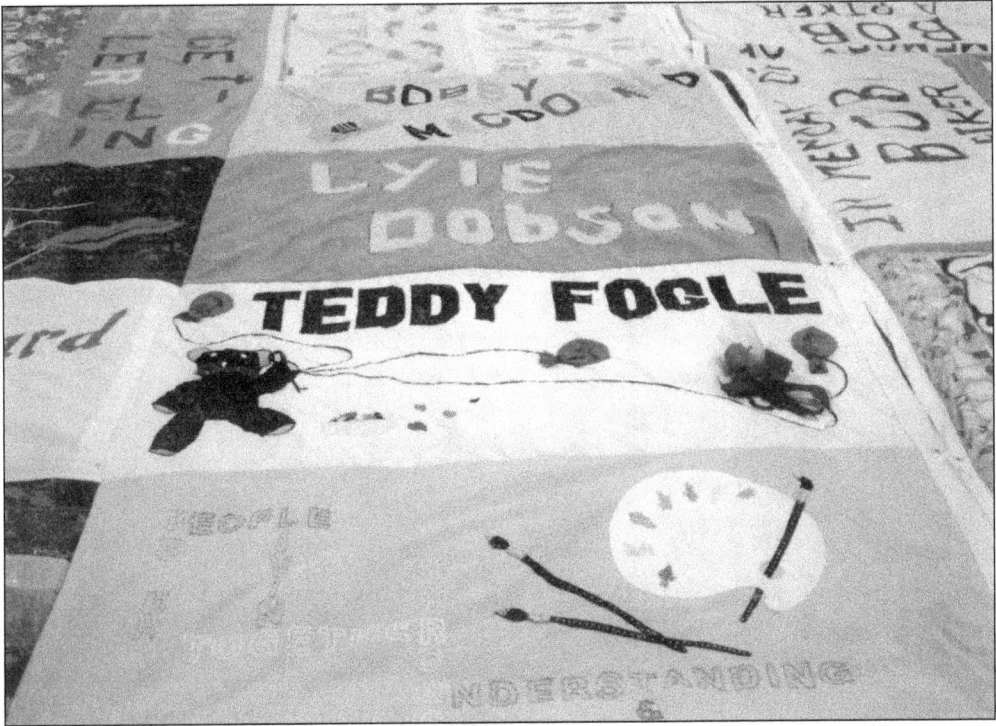

TEDDY FOGLE AIDS MEMORIAL QUILT PANEL, OCTOBER 11, 1987. The AIDS Memorial Quilt was conceived by San Francisco activist Cleve Jones in 1985. The quilt was first displayed on October 11, 1987, and included 1,920 panels. Shown here is the panel of Teddy Fogle (above), one of the Richmonders among those memorialized that day on the National Mall. The public response to the quilt was positive and immediate and led to a 20-city national tour in the summer of 1988. When the quilt returned to D.C. for a second time in October 1988, it had grown to over 8,000 panels. In 1989, a second tour of the quilt was completed. By 1992, the AIDS Memorial Quilt (right) contained panels from all 50 states and 28 countries. The last full display of the quilt was in October 1996.

METROPOLITAN COMMUNITY CHURCH AT RICHMOND PRIDE, OCTOBER 1992. Supporters of the Metropolitan Community Church (MCC) of Richmond gather at the Richmond Pride Festival in October 1992. MCC of Richmond intends to meet the spiritual needs of gays and lesbians. They held their first worship services on July 9, 1978, at the Friends Meeting House at 4500 Kensington Avenue. The MCC moved to the corner of Park and Davis Avenues in February 1993. On January 29, 1989, MCC participated in an ecumenical service at St. Mark's Episcopal Church, where AIDS Memorial Quilt panels were presented and displayed. The "Richmond Panel" commemorated the lives of the 75 known persons who had died of AIDS in Richmond as of January 1989. The panel included the names of Jim Isbell, Stacy Schulze, Teddy Fogle, Doug Jones, and Al Johnson. When he died on October 17, 1991, Leon "Harvey" Johnson (left) became the first casualty of AIDS served by the Richmond AIDS Ministry (RAM) organization.

Three

LIVING OUT

TRACY THORNE, C. 1992. On May 19, 1992, Oceana, Virginia–based navy lieutenant Tracy Thorne appeared on ABC's *Nightline* and announced he was gay. He urged the military to end the "Don't Ask, Don't Tell" policy, which required gays and lesbians to keep secret their sexual orientation lest they be involuntarily discharged. After the television pronouncement, Thorne's career stalled, and in May 1995, he was honorably discharged. Thorne challenged his discharge in court. After a series of prolonged legal appeals, the U.S. Supreme Court refused to hear his claim that the military's policy violated his free speech rights. Thorne was not the first person in the armed services to challenge the military's gay ban and certainly not the only gay to be discharged. Leonard Matlovich (1943–1988) protested the military's stance, too, following his discharge in 1975. From 1994 to 2001, over 7,000 service personnel were forced out of the military because of the "Don't Ask, Don't Tell" policy. Thorne is now an assistant commonwealth's attorney in Richmond.

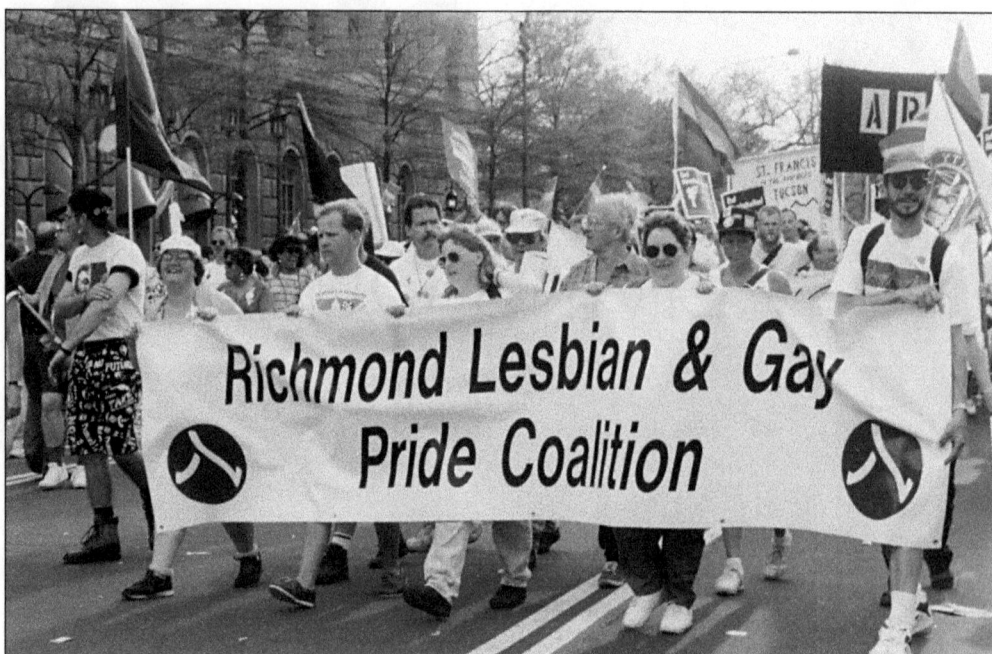

RICHMOND LESBIAN AND GAY PRIDE COALITION IN D.C., APRIL 25, 1993. Richmonders at the 1993 National March on Washington for Lesbian, Gay and Bisexual Rights and Liberation in Washington, D.C., hold the banner for the Richmond Lesbian and Gay Pride Coalition. The Richmond Lesbian and Gay Pride Coalition began in 1987. Virginians for Gay Rights holds a banner in the photograph below. (Both courtesy Bob Swisher Papers.)

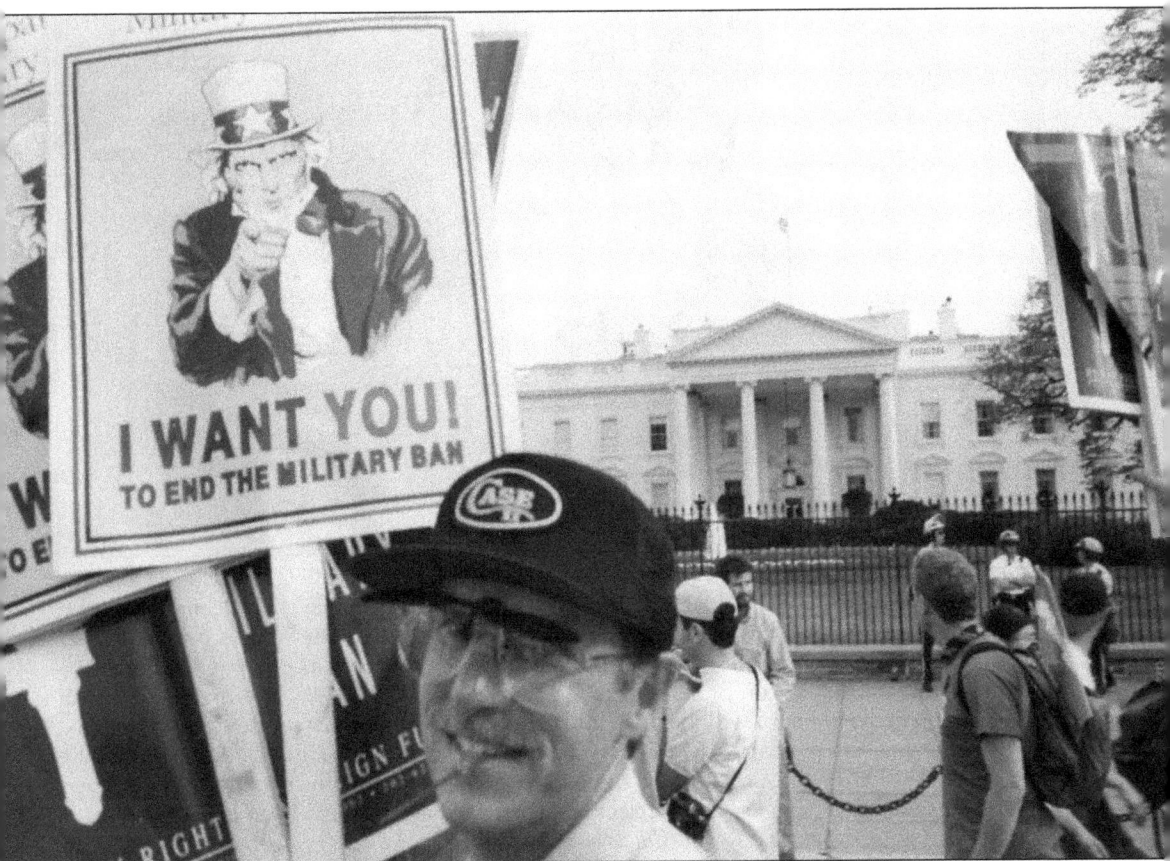

BOB SWISHER AT THE MARCH ON WASHINGTON, 1993. A prominent political issue at the time of the 1993 March on Washington was ending the ban on homosexuals in the U.S. Armed Forces. While campaigning for president in 1992, Bill Clinton had promised to allow all citizens regardless of sexual orientation to serve openly in the armed forces. This was a departure from the long-standing ban on homosexuals in the military. Once elected, Clinton was met with opposition from both political parties and had to compromise on the issue. The compromise became known as "Don't Ask, Don't Tell," meaning the military will discharge a soldier who engages in homosexual conduct, admits to being gay, or attempts to marry someone of the same sex. (Courtesy Bob Swisher Papers.)

RICHMOND TRIANGLE PLAYERS ACTORS, NOVEMBER 1994. Begun in 1992 by Michael Gooding, Steve Earle, and Marcus Miller, the Richmond Triangle Players made their debut with a trio of one-act plays based on Harvey Fierstein's *Safe Sex Trilogy*. The performances benefited local AIDS projects. The shows on November 4, 6, and 7, 1992, were performed to a full house in the upstairs theater at Fieldens on Broad Street. The first play, *Manny & Jake*, was directed by Jacqui Singleton and starred Paul Daddona and Bill Baron. The next two plays were *Safe Sex* directed by Gooding and starring Earle and John Gorman and *Forget Him* starring Gooding and Miller and directed by Earle. The success of the three shows convinced Gooding to continue the theater troupe. In 2007, the Triangle Players celebrated their 15th anniversary. Seen here are actors of *Elegies for Angels, Punks, and Raging Queens*.

VIRGINIANS FOR JUSTICE. Supporters of Virginians for Justice march down West Cary Street during the Gay Pride Festival on September 22, 1996. Founded in 1989, Virginians for Justice (VJ) was the forerunner of Equality Virginia, the statewide political lobby and education organization for lesbians, gays, transgenders, bisexuals, and their straight allies. Virginians for Justice sought to educate the public on issues of importance to LGBTs, track local hate crimes, and repeal the state code's sodomy law. The group also sponsored a lobbyist at the Virginia General Assembly during each session of the 1990s and fought for the rights of gay and lesbian families. In 2002, the lobby group reorganized and became known as Equality Virginia.

SHIRLEY LESSER AT GAY PRIDE, SEPTEMBER 1993. Shirley Lesser was an advocate, prominent spokesperson, and executive director of Virginians for Justice. She was instrumental in establishing the Hate Crimes Hotline through VJ. Lesser also was a founding member of the Richmond Lesbian and Gay Pride Coalition, a former writer for the *Richmond Pride*, and a spokesperson for the Richmond Lesbian and Gay Alliance.

GAY AND LESBIAN ACTIVISTS AT A PARTY, 1993. During the 1990s, several fund-raising parties for the Richmond Lesbian and Gay Pride Coalition and Virginians for Justice were held at Carl Archacki's house. Standing in this photograph were, from left to right, David Northrup, Patrick Heck, Beth Marschak, Bob Rogers, David Perry, Mary Gay Hutcherson, Yoli Farnum, and Shirley Lesser. All were members and leaders of several LGBT organizations in Richmond.

SHARON BOTTOMS (LEFT) AND HER PARTNER APRIL WADE, 1994. In March 1993, Bottoms lost custody of her son, Tyler, in a court decision that made national press. Bottoms's mother filed for custody claiming that her daughter, a lesbian, was unfit to be a parent. Bottoms expended many legal appeals with legal counsel provided by the Virginia ACLU. She finally gave up the custody battle for her son in 1996. Bottoms eventually earned visitation rights but only if Wade was not present. Before Bottoms's case, many lesbians had lost custody cases in Virginia family courts, but few people knew about the plight of these "Jane Does." In family court, no record was kept of the proceedings and the specifics of the decisions were kept private. Bottoms's case was different because she appealed the decision to a higher court and used her own name. (Courtesy *Richmond Times-Dispatch*.)

SHARON BOTTOMS (LEFT) AND APRIL WADE IN NEW YORK CITY, JUNE 26, 1994. Sharon Bottoms's custody case energized lesbians, gays, and their organizations to speak out in support of LGBT families in new ways. In September 1993, Bottoms and Wade participated in Richmond Lesbian and Gay Pride. There was a large turnout because people were upset about the precedent this case established with respect to lesbian and gay families. Many people in Virginia, both LGBT and straight, were appalled at the court's decision to take a child from his mother. In this photograph, Bottoms and Wade marched in New York City to commemorate the 25th anniversary of the Stonewall Inn riots.

LESBIAN PROTESTERS AT RICHMOND PRIDE, SEPTEMBER 12, 1993. The Sharon Bottoms custody case was fresh on the minds of Lesbian and Gay Pride Festival participants in September 1993. The parade marchers displayed several protest messages, including this family who wore paper-bag masks and a banner. A sign in the background of this photograph notes "Where is Mary Sue?" The message refers to Mary Sue Terry, then Virginia attorney general and Democratic candidate for governor. Many people expected Terry's campaign to establish a strong platform for lesbian and gay rights. As a single woman in politics, Terry faced a "whisper campaign," a false rumor that she was endorsed by lesbian and gay groups and was a lesbian.

Lesbian Women of Color (LWOC) is a social/political organization founded to provide support for Lesbians of color.

For further information, call or write: 804/359-39.. LWOC - P.O. Box 945 Richmond, Va 23207-094.

LESBIAN WOMEN OF COLOR FLYER, 1993. Lesbian Women of Color (later Lesbian Womyn of Color) was organized by Terri Pendleton in the early 1990s. The group provided a range of activities from potlucks and raps to teas and dances. In 1993, they cosponsored a fund-raiser for Sharon Bottoms at Club Colours. Located at 536 North Harrison Street, Club Colours always has reserved certain nights for the LGBT crowd. After Lesbian Womyn of Color disbanded, several of their members started another African American women's group called Gatekeepers. Around this time, an African American gay men's group started, too.

CAMPOUT WOMEN, C. 1995. Beth Marschak (left) and another volunteer are seen here selling T-shirts and registering CampOut members for W4 (Wild Western Women's Weekend) around 1995. W4 typically included country-and-western dance classes, country music performers, and the Crazy Feats Rodeo. The women of CampOut built the cabin in the photograph along with the other structures, showers, and a kitchen on this rural property. The women even cleared land for a lake on the property. Richmond Lesbian-Feminists also provided funding and some of the volunteer labor to build the open-air dance pavilion. The CampOut logo is seen in the photograph below.

www.campoutva.com

CRAZY FEATS RODEO AT CAMPOUT W4, 2003. The winning team poses after the Crazy Feats Rodeo at the CampOut W4 on Labor Day Weekend 2003. CampOut is a private, women-owned and -operated campground for women midway between Richmond and Charlottesville. Originally known as InTouch, the campground started in the late 1980s and later changed ownership and name. This group has provided a women's space for camping as well as a venue for events like the Virginia Women's Music Festival. Many lesbians, bisexual, and straight women have been among the members.

WOMEN'S SOFTBALL AT HUMPHREY-CALDER FIELD, MID-1990S. Since the 1940s, playing and watching women's sports has been an important social activity for the lesbian community. This was true of bowling, soccer, rugby, and flag football. But softball usually drew the largest crowd. Sporting events provided a social space for lesbians unable to afford the high-end, private parties available to the wealthy. The league was open to all women, and teams included many straight players, too. Players and fans often went to Babe's following the games.

WOMEN'S SOFTBALL PROTEST AT CITY HALL, LATE 1990S. Richmond Metro Women's Sports Association (RMWSA) members stood for this photograph in city hall, pausing before going to a Richmond City Council meeting. At the meeting, the women spoke in opposition to a city decision to exclude women's softball play at Humphrey-Calder. In the late 1990s, the city decided that this field would no longer be available to the women's teams and instead would become a Little League field. The Metro Richmond Women's Sports Association was organized to fight this decision and to provide information and support for women's sports in the area.

THE VIRGINIA GayZette

THE LESBIAN, GAY & BISEXUAL NEWSPAPER FOR THE REST OF US.

Premier Issue / October 1999

Behold! A paper is born
by Kirk Read, former Editor of OUR OWN COMMUNITY PRESS

Yee haw, kids. The Virginia GayZette is born. Please direct all frankincense, gold, and myrrh to the staff. As you know, one can never have enough myrrh.

This is your paper, and keeping it alive and well is up to each and every one of you. Community activism and goodwill kept Our Own alive for 22 years. Here's hoping that you will nurture this paper into the next millennium.

What can you do to keep the Gayzette in print?

Read it faithfully. If the only thing you do is pick up the paper and read it, you've contributed to its survival. A newspaper must have an audience. Pick up every LGBT publication you can find. When a community is lucky enough to have multiple papers, it's a sign of growth. Different publications serve different functions, markets, and audiences. If Virginia can embrace multiple papers without seeing them as competitors, our community will have an opportunity to flourish.

Talk it up to friends.
Pick up extra copies and pass them around.

Join the team. Here's a typical scenario: a person looks at the paper, doesn't see an event or community covered adequately. That person throws down the paper, gripes to their friends, and never looks at the paper again. Nothing changes.

Alternative scenario: a person picks up the paper, sees a need for improvement, and contacts the paper by letter or email. In helpful, team-oriented language, that person makes suggestions and comments.

Say "I'll help out by sending you information on what our group is up to." Or "I'd like to write for you." Or "I'll sell ads." Or "I'll proof-read." Or "I'll sell ads." Or "I'll deliver papers." Or "I'll take pictures." If you have a pulse, you have something to offer. Come forward and make your voice heard.

"I will" is a much more powerful way to start a sentence than "Y'all screwed up."

Respect the Gayzette team. All too often, we trash our community leaders when we disagree with them or when they aren't doing things we think ought to be done. Remember that many of these folks are either volunteers or paid very little. They do community work because they care about making Virginia a safe and fair (and fun!) place for LGBT people.

When you see Gayzette staffers or other community workers out and about, thank them even if you don't know them. Take a moment to write them supportive email and letters. There were times during my tenure at Out Own that a single letter or phone call made all the difference in the world. One production week at 3AM, I was pulling my hair out, wondering why I was making less than minimum wage. An email came in from a 16-year-old girl who found the paper and decided not to cut her wrists. That was enough for me to continue.

continued on page 2

Ed Harris (Ministry Virginia), Senator John Edwards, David Perry (Virginians For Justice) at this years Pride In The Park X

Roanoke Celebrates "Pride In The Park X"
by Ed Harris

The Pride Kick-Off Show, hosted by "The Park," entertained in two shows to a packed house on Friday evening, September 17th, to begin the weekend of Pride In The Park X. Both the current Miss Gay Roanoke and the current and past Mr. Gay Roanoke were among the featured entertainers.

Saturday evening the Community Auction was held at the Unitarian Universalist Church, featuring items for every budget, free appetizers and drinks, also hosting a "packed house." The auction is always a great social time as well as a wonderful fund-raising event for the Gay Pride weekend!

Sunday's park festival had a crowd of over 1000 attending. There were more than 30 vendors present selling food, drinks and merchandise as well as various organizations providing information booths. There was a pet refreshment station that included a veterinarian and two group offered Harley rides. This year there was also an anonymous HIV testing station.

This stage entertainment included the musical talents of The Terry Day & Tony James Band, Morphy Blue, and Radar Rose. Guest speakers included Sam Garrison and Senator John Edwards. The Rogues L/LC performed "Proud, Strong & United," encouraging crowd participation. The Fellowship Bowling League "Nuns" performed their rendition of "Ain't No Mountain High Enough" and "I Will Follow Him," from the "Sister Act" movies.

This year's Lambda Service Award was given posthumously to Walt Blouch and the Community Service Award was presented to The Rogues.

In honor of the tenth anniversary of Pride In The Park, the PIP X Committee chose to donate to several community organizations. The recipients were: the Blue Ridge Lambda Press $200, Blue Ridge AIDS Support Services $200, Parents, Families and Friends of Lesbians and Gays (PFLAG) of Roanoke/Roanoke Valley $100 for the Walt Blouch Scholarship Fund, Metropolitan Community Church of the Blue Ridge $100, The Rogues L/LC for their charitable causes $100 and The Fellowship League to sponsor a family for Christmas $100.

Inside this Edition: Learn about the history of GAY PRIDE Richmond Style!
(see page 6)

VIRGINIA GAYZETTE AND OUT & ABOUT. With the final issue of *Our Own Community Press* still on the minds of gay Virginians, the *Virginia GayZette* began publishing monthly in October 1999 to fill the information void left by the newspaper. While *Out & About of Virginia* principally covered the gay social scene, the *Virginia GayZette* provided gay and lesbian Virginians with relevant information about news as it pertained to them. The *GayZette* was published by Phoenix Rising owners Rex Mitchell and Jim Todd. The newspaper ceased publishing in 2005.

October - 2002

Out And About Of Virginia

Heath Ledger On The Way To The Top!

Richmond Shows Pride

Comic Kevin Meany Cruising For VJ

Unity Raises $9,000

TRANSGENDERS AT RICHMOND PRIDE, SEPTEMBER 22, 1996. In this photograph, transgenders parade through Carytown at Richmond Pride in 1996. Richmond's trans community is a broad one, encompassing people with many forms of gender expression. Their expressions have varied from drag queen and drag king to those who are male-to-female (MTF) and female-to-male (FTM) or in transition. Trans people have expressed gender in visible, nontraditional ways and have suffered as frequent targets of hate speech and violence. (Many of the people who were harassed and arrested at the Stonewall Inn riots in New York City in 1969 were transgender.) Support organizations like Virginia's Secrets and the Richmond Transformers began in part to help trans people cope with these issues. The Fan Free Clinic also has provided a health clinic for MTF and FTM people and space for support groups.

OTHER VOICES CHORUS, SEPTEMBER 14, 1997. Photographed at the Carillon in Byrd Park during the Richmond Gay Pride Festival, Other Voices Chorus was founded in 1991. The group strived to affirm the gay experience through choral music. They often performed at gay and lesbian events but disbanded in the late 1990s. Other Voices was not the first gay choral group in Richmond. The Richmond Gay Men's Chorus and the Dignity/Integrity chorus performed in the 1980s.

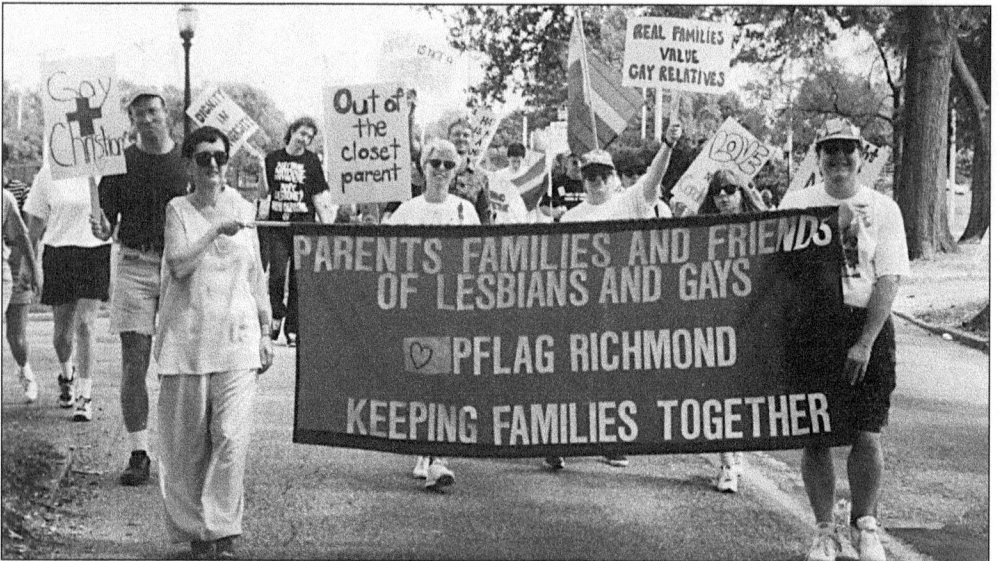

PFLAG MARCHES AT GAY PRIDE, SEPTEMBER 14, 1997. Founded in 1994, the Richmond chapter of Parents and Families of Lesbians and Gays (PFLAG) has worked to advocate for, support, and educate LGBT people and their families. Other organizations, like Gay and Lesbian Student Education Network (GLSEN), also work in Richmond to improve lives of students and families. GLSEN Richmond had its first chapter meeting on January 29, 2000. Among its many activities and goals, GLSEN combats harassment and discrimination leveled against students and school personnel. They also work to establish and support gay-straight alliances in schools.

MOMS AND KIDS HOLIDAY PARTY, MID-1990S. This image depicts "Sister Santa" and her elf assistant at a Moms and Kids Holiday Party held at the Richmond Friends Meeting House. Richmond Lesbian-Feminists held this event for many years, sometimes cosponsoring with groups like Metropolitan Community Church. The event was one of several activities that RLF organized to give gay and lesbian families a chance to socialize. The program included games, refreshments, and singing. Adults brought gifts for the children. After each child had a chance to talk to sister Santa, a friendly elf helped Santa pass out the gifts.

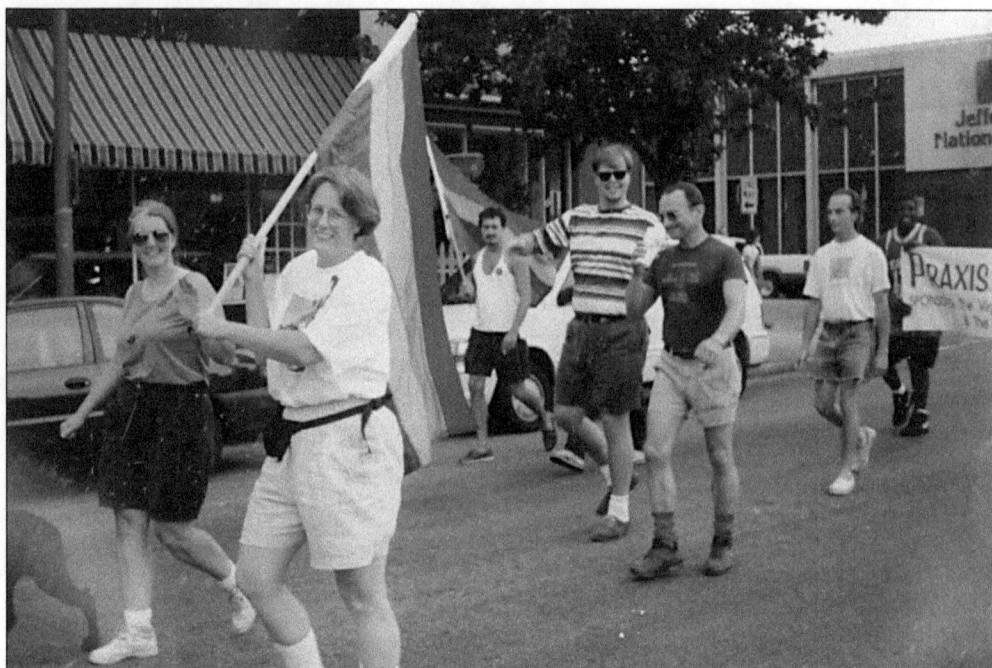

GAY PRIDE FESTIVAL AND PARADE, SEPTEMBER 1995. In this photograph, from left to right, Chris Clarke, Kathy Benham, Marc Purintun, and Larry Koontz march through Carytown with other festival-goers during the 1995 Lesbian and Gay Pride Parade. They are walking in front of Babe's of Carytown, a lesbian bar at 3166 West Cary Street owned by Vicky Hester. Opened in 1979, Babe's is the oldest existing LGBT-friendly bar in Richmond.

FIELDENS. Fieldens is a private, after-hours club located at 2033 West Broad Street that has provided an activity venue for dance, theater, and the arts for several years. The upstairs theater served as the site for Richmond Triangle Players productions since their first play in 1992. Like other gay bars and restaurants in Richmond, Fieldens has supported Lesbian and Gay Pride and other LGBT events.

GROUP AT CHRISTOPHER'S, APRIL 11, 1993. After the Easter Parade, a group gets together at Christopher's, a gay bar in Carytown at 2811 West Cary Street. Carytown is another lesbigay-friendly area, home to many lesbian or gay restaurants and bars over the years. With its eclectic mix of shops and street performers, Carytown is one of the prime people-watching spots in Richmond. On the right is a photograph of the Carytown Inn, a former gay hangout located at 3028 West Cary Street. (Right, courtesy Taylor Dabney.)

BARCODE (FORMERLY CASABLANCA). In the 1990s, this site at 6 East Grace Street housed Casablanca, a gay restaurant and bar. Now owned by Richmond Triangle Players founder Marcus Miller, the Barcode has occupied the site for the last several years. Aside from providing food, drink, and entertainment, the restaurant and bar also has supported local gay and lesbian events like Gay Pride.

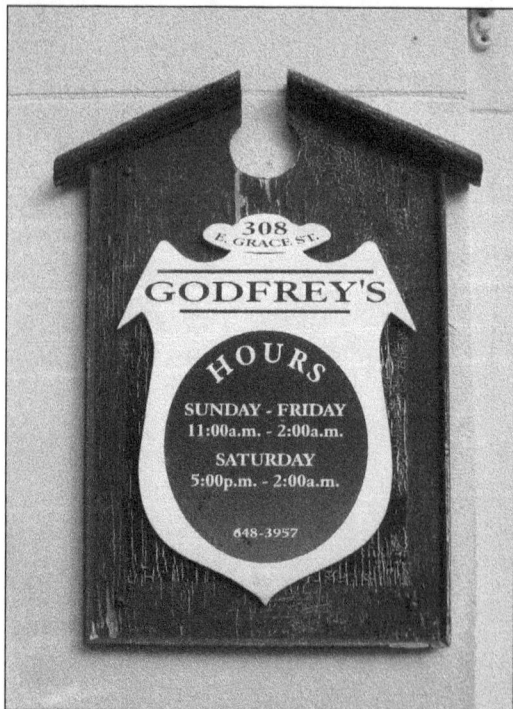

GODFREY'S. Famous for their Sunday Drag Brunch, which has attracted a wide audience of straights and gays for many years, Godfrey's is located at 301 East Grace Street. This restaurant and bar offers music and a large dance floor. Jeff Willis, both a drag show promoter and participant, is one of the owners and has been active over the years with many community events, including Pride.

TABER'S, 1978. Taber's was owned by Donald Taber and located at Second and Grace Streets. Some of the other LGBT restaurants and bars from past days include Alexander's (3129 West Cary Street), the Cha-Cha Palace (719 West Broad Street), and the Pyramid (1008 North Boulevard Avenue). Scandals (briefly known as Rumours) was a popular locale for gays, too, particularly in the 1980s. (Courtesy Taylor Dabney.)

MARY DEAN CARTER AND BETH MARSCHAK, 1993. Mary Dean Carter (left) and Beth Marschak, both longtime members of Richmond Lesbian-Feminists and graduates of Westhampton College, pause for a photograph at Richmond's Monument Avenue Easter Parade. Walking the avenue and its wide median while enjoying live music is a tradition at this Fan District event, where the people are the parade. The Fan District is one of the very LGBT-friendly areas of Richmond.

MARY GAY HUTCHERSON AND YOLANDA FARNUM. Mary Gay Hutcherson (with wedding program) and Yolanda "Yoli" Farnum held their wedding at Metropolitan Community Church (MCC) on February 14, 2000. The couple also participated in the mass wedding at the 2000 Millennium March on Washington, had commitment ceremonies on the several ocean cruises, and was legally married in Provincetown, Massachusetts, in October 2005. Both women were active in various women's and LGBT organizations, including Equality Virginia and Make Love Legal. Hutcherson also volunteered time for the Richmond Lesbian-Feminists, Women Books, and Richmond Organization for Sexual Minority Youth. She also sponsored a gay student alliance at James River High School, where she worked. Hutcherson frequently answered the RLF phone line, helping new residents learn about LGBT activities. Mentioning Mary Gay's name was a coded way to find out if someone else was "family."

JACQUI SINGLETON ON NEW YEAR'S EVE, 2000. Jacqui Singleton (above, on right) and her band perform for revelers (below) at Richmond Lesbian-Feminists' New Year's Eve Celebration in 2000. Richmond Lesbian-Feminists have organized New Year's celebrations for many years, starting in member's homes and moving to the Bon Air Community Center in the early 1990s. As a singer-songwriter, Singleton has been a performer at Richmond area LGBT events for many years. She was frequently featured at Richmond Pride festivals. Singleton also has written and directed many screenplays, including *Manny and Jake*, the first Richmond Triangle Players production in 1992. Singleton's Jera Productions company has produced a number of plays with a lesbian focus. She also has authored several published lesbian novels.

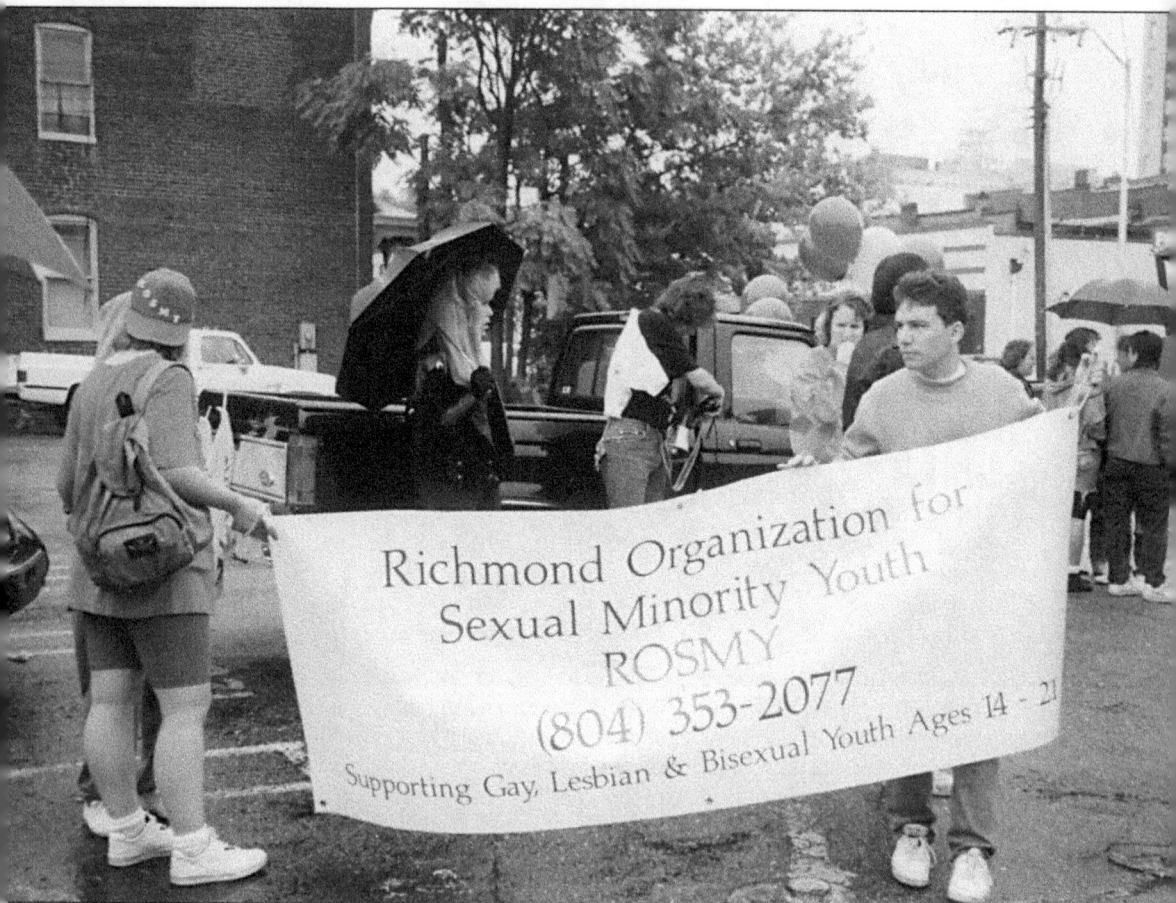

ROSMY Prior to Gay Pride Parade, 1997. In the late 1980s, Jon Klein (far right) worked on the Richmond Street Outreach Project, distributing free needles and condoms to drug users and prostitutes while educating them on the spread of HIV. In 1991, he and Chris Clarke helped found the Richmond Organization for Sexual Minority Youth (ROSMY). Klein served as its first executive director. ROSMY is one of the oldest continuous organizations serving to enhance the well-being of LGBT youth in the country. Klein founded Diversity Thrift in August 2000. Owned and operated by the Richmond Gay Community Foundation (RGCF), a nonprofit organization that seeks to improve the lives of LGBTs through funding and education, Diversity Thrift is the principal fund-raising organization of the RGCF. Some of their beneficiaries have included the Fan Free Clinic and the Richmond Triangle Players.

JUDD PROCTOR, C. 1996. Public schoolteacher Judd Proctor started a support group for gay, lesbian, and bisexual Virginia educators as an opportunity to exchange information on topics like sexual minority youth, the National Education Association's Gay and Lesbian Caucus, and other LGBT issues relevant to educators. The group, later named the Virginia Gay, Lesbian, and Bisexual Educators Association, first met at Proctor's home on September 18, 1993. The meeting attracted 100 educators. A second gathering in February 1994 had an attendance of about 75. The short-lived organization last met in October 1994. Proctor continued to advocate for educators' rights, sexual minority youth, and gay rights in general. Since 2005, Proctor and his partner, Brian Burns, have produced the "Rainbow Minute," a weekday 60-second blurb about gay history and culture recorded at WRIR radio in Richmond.

Two Friends at Festival Park, Mid-1990s. For some people, Pride events were a chance to protest and speak out. For other people, the festivals were an opportunity to camp it up a bit, as these two friends are doing in Festival Park in the mid-1990s.

Leather Group at Richmond Pride, Mid-1990s. As in most cities, Richmond has a leather club tradition dating back many years. The Teddy Bear Leather Club has a long history of assisting at Pride events and often served as marshals for the parades. They also have a long tradition of generously raising money for many charitable causes.

BANNER AT RICHMOND PRIDE, 1997. This photograph depicts several people assembled and holding a banner prior to the Richmond Pride Parade through Carytown in September 1997. ROBIN, the Richmond Bisexual Network, was founded in 1993 as an affiliate of the national organization BiNet USA. Bisexuals have been a part of Richmond LGBT organizations since the beginning. Richmond Lesbian-Feminists, as an example, was for women-identified-women, which could include bisexual women and straight feminists. In the 1970s, many lesbian and gay groups included bisexual members, although some members felt that bisexuality was a "phase" and that eventually the person would come out as lesbian or gay. For these reasons, bisexuals did not feel welcomed and wanted their own organizations.

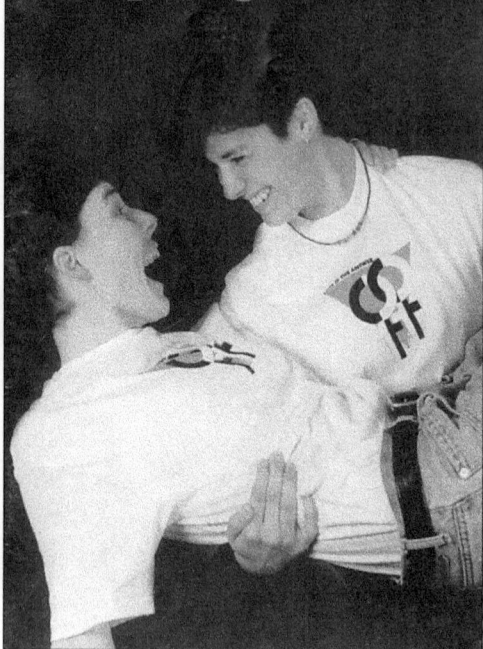

PHOENIX RISING, 1995. Located at 19 North Belmont in Carytown, Phoenix Rising was begun in 1993 as an independent bookstore with media and other materials of interest to LGBTs. Owned by Jim Todd and Rex Mitchell, the business soon became a popular location for placing information about LGBT activities. The store included local and regional newspapers and a bulletin board to help connect LGBTs with one another. Below is a Sharon Bottoms and April Wade Defense Fund jar, which was placed in the store during the couple's legal custody fight.

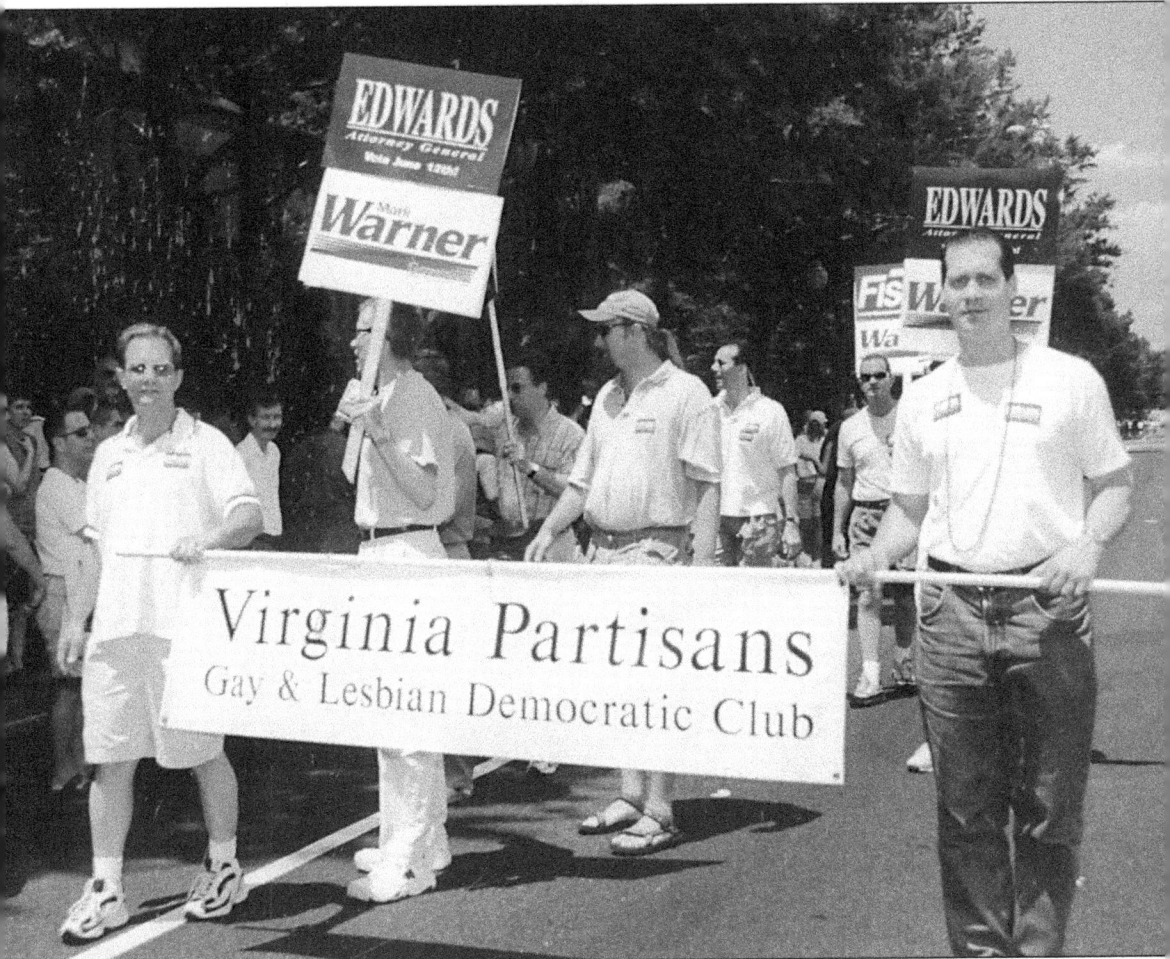

VIRGINIA PARTISANS GAY AND LESBIAN DEMOCRATIC CLUB, 2001. The Virginia Partisans Gay and Lesbian Democratic Club marched in D.C. in 2001 prior to the November elections. The Partisans were not the first Democratic LGBT group in Virginia. Earlier there was an informal Richmond group that organized and hosted a LGBT hospitality suite at the party's Virginia conventions. The Partisans sprung from an informal group that organized a fund-raiser in 1990 for Congressman Jim Moran's first congressional campaign. The group continued to meet and formally organized, elected officers, and adopted bylaws in 1992. Today they continue to lobby for LGBT reforms. The Log Cabin Republicans also have an active and growing chapter in Virginia. They were founded in 1997. (Courtesy Lana R. Lawrence.)

ADAM EBBIN, 2001. Adam Ebbin is the first openly gay member of the Virginia General Assembly, representing the 49th District in Northern Virginia. Elected in 2003, Ebbin ran unopposed in 2005 and defeated an Independent candidate in 2007 to earn his third term in office. Ebbin has lobbied and worked at the general assembly in Richmond for many years, including as former president of the Virginia Partisans. Ebbin was the third openly gay elected official in Virginia. In 2006, Arlington County School Board member Sally Baird became the first openly lesbian elected official in Virginia. (Courtesy Lana R. Lawrence.)

VIOLA BASKERVILLE. Beginning in 1994 with her election to Richmond City Council, Baskerville advocated for LGBTs and frequently attended LGBT events. In 1997, she won election to the Virginia House of Delegates. As delegate, she spoke in opposition to the Marriage Affirmation Act and the Marshall-Newman Amendment and was instrumental in cosponsoring pro-LGBT legislation. She left the general assembly in 2005 and campaigned for the Democratic nomination for lieutenant governor (the first African American woman to run). In 2006, Gov. Tim Kaine appointed Baskerville as secretary of the administration. During her acceptance speech for the Equality Virginia Award in 2007, Baskerville noted: "Now that Virginia has written discrimination into our state Constitution, it will take a concerted, broad-based coalition to erase it. I stand here tonight as a representative of two other minorities to urge those who look like me to join in this fight by speaking out for human rights and human dignity."

MARK WARNER SPEAKS TO THE VIRGINIA PARTISANS, 2001. As more LGBTs became active politically in the 1990s, Virginia politicians began to expend campaign resources on them as constituents. The formation of Equality Virginia (formerly Virginians for Justice), the Virginia Partisans, and the Log Cabin Republicans strengthened the power of the LGBT movement to lobby their political agenda. The effectiveness of the LGBT lobby helped gain inclusion of "sexual orientation" in Mark Warner's (and Tim Kaine's) executive orders concerning anti-discrimination. The "gay vote" also played a role in recent election results, particularly in Northern Virginia. (Courtesy Lana R. Lawrence.)

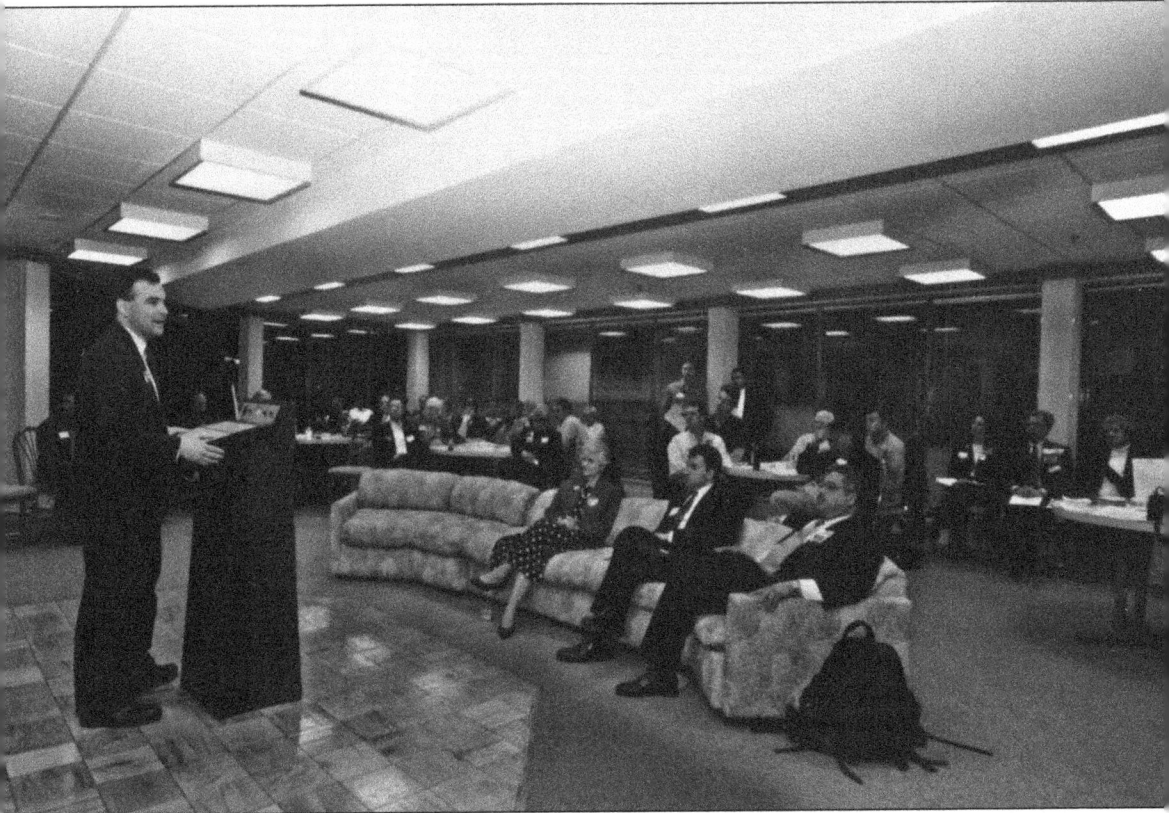

TIM KAINE CAMPAIGNS FOR LIEUTENANT GOVERNOR, 2001. Tim Kaine was elected lieutenant governor in 2001 and then governor in 2005. On January 14, 2006, his first day in office, Governor Kaine signed Executive Order No. 1. The action specifically prolonged Governor Warner's addition of sexual orientation to the government's anti-discrimination policy. Warner quietly added sexual orientation to the government's equal employment opportunity policy via executive order on December 16, 2005, a month before leaving office. The Code of Virginia does not include sexual orientation as a protected class in its equal employment policy. (Courtesy Lana R. Lawrence.)

TIM KAINE SPEAKS TO THE VIRGINIA PARTISANS, 2001. Tim Kaine spoke to this group of Virginia Partisans during his campaign for lieutenant governor in 2001. He was elected to that office, serving under Gov. Mark Warner. Four years later, Kaine won the office of governor of Virginia. LGBTs in Virginia voted for Kaine in large numbers in that election. In April 2006, Governor Kaine agreed to vote "no" against the proposed Marshall-Newman Amendment. (Courtesy Lana R. Lawrence.)

BRIAN BURNS AND JUDD PROCTOR, 1996. In 2006, Brian Burns and Judd Proctor were married in Massachusetts, a state that recognizes same-sex marriages. The Marriage Affirmation Act (House Bill 751) disallowed gay marriage in Virginia and stated, "A civil union, partnership contract, or other arrangement between persons of the same sex purporting to bestow the privileges or obligations or marriage is prohibited. Any such civil union, partnership contract or other arrangement entered into by persons of the same sex in another state or jurisdiction shall be void in all respects in Virginia and any contractual rights created thereby shall be void and unenforceable." While their marriage certificate is not legally recognized in Virginia, Proctor and Burns's act represents the couple's personal commitment and the resilience of many gay and lesbian families to advocate on their behalf while living in a state that does not recognize their partnership.

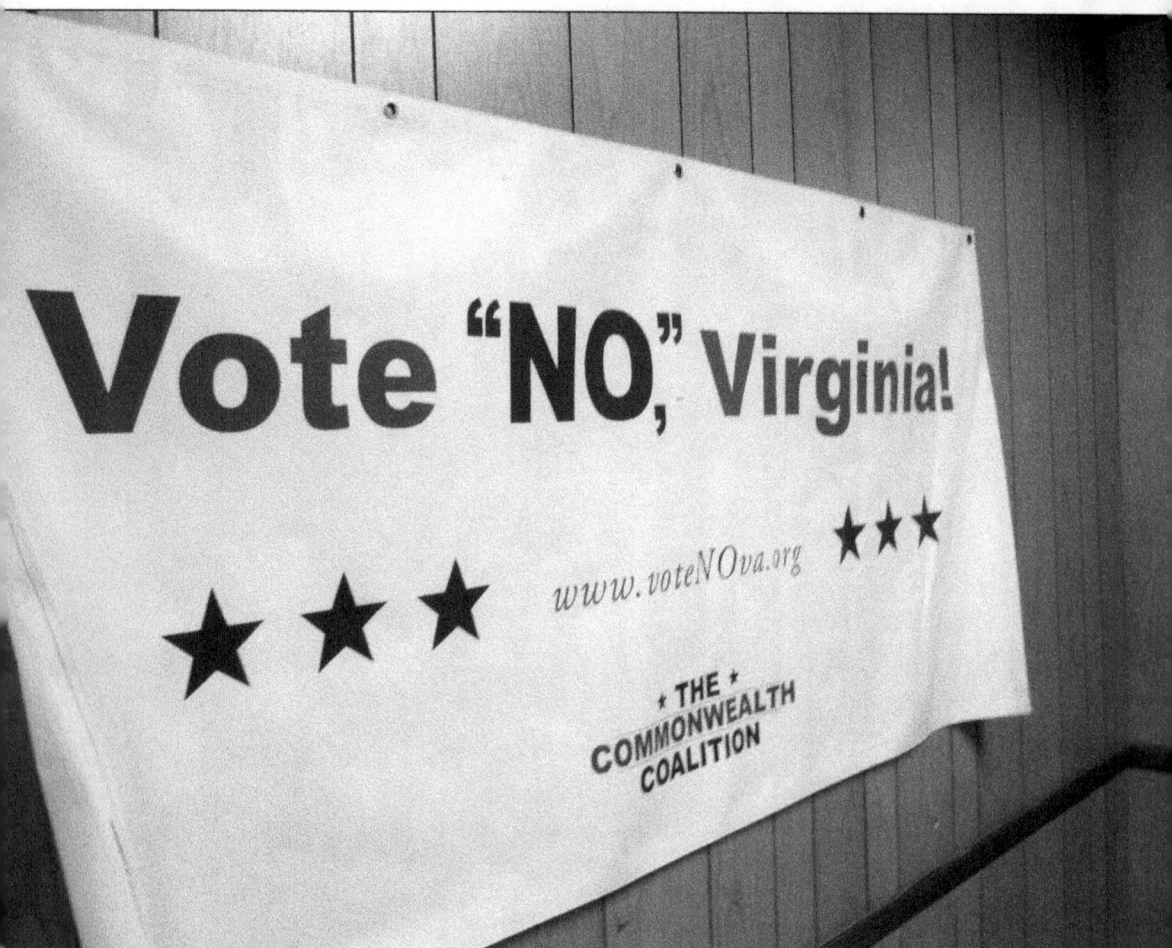

COMMONWEALTH COALITION, 2006. The Commonwealth Coalition was a nonpartisan alliance of organizations and individuals whose goal was the defeat of the amendment to the Virginia Bill of Rights proposed by Delegate Bob Marshall and Sen. Steve Newman. The Virginia General Assembly already had passed the Marriage Affirmation Act (House Bill 751), effective July 1, 2004, which prohibited same-sex marriages and unions. The Marshall-Newman Amendment broadened that act and proposed a ban on legal recognition of unmarried relationships, gay or straight, that "approximate the design, qualities, significance, or effects of marriage." The coalition's campaign was led by Claire Guthrie Gastañaga and launched April 8, 2006.

LGBT Supporters at the Virginia State Capitol, January 25, 2006. Equality Virginia supporters have participated in "Lobby Day" at the Virginia General Assembly for the past several years. Virginians for Justice, the forerunner of Equality Virginia, and their supporters began attending Lobby Day in the 1990s. In this photograph, several hundred proponents of the "Vote No" campaign pose following their lobbying efforts against the Marshall-Newman Amendment. Virginia voters ratified the amendment in the November 7, 2006, election, but turnout from "no" voters was significant. Their participation in the election was in part credited with the defeat of incumbent Republican U.S. senator George Allen by Democrat James Webb.

ACROSS AMERICA, PEOPLE ARE DISCOVERING SOMETHING WONDERFUL. *THEIR HERITAGE.*

Arcadia Publishing is the leading local history publisher in the United States. With more than 4,000 titles in print and hundreds of new titles released every year, Arcadia has extensive specialized experience chronicling the history of communities and celebrating America's hidden stories, bringing to life the people, places, and events from the past. To discover the history of other communities across the nation, please visit:

www.arcadiapublishing.com

Customized search tools allow you to find regional history books about the town where you grew up, the cities where your friends and family live, the town where your parents met, or even that retirement spot you've been dreaming about.

MAP SEARCH